TRACKING WITH ANGELS

Twelve Adventure stories
in the series:
Tracking with Angels

❧

Barton R Thom

ISBN: 9780991347735

Cover painting by Carol Bourdo of Trinidad, Colorado
Cover design Interior design by Reality Info
though Elance

Dedicated to
GOD,

My Guardian Angel Dancing Hawk,
And
The Lakota Medicine Man Dan Wilde
Who taught me how to
Track with Angels

I want to thank my daughter for every day that we spent tracking together with Dan Wilde. I cherish every memory.

I want to give a special thanks for the encouragement and assistance of Paul Gray of Albuquerque, NM.

Books by Barton R Thom in the series

TRACKING WITH ANGELS

Tracking with Angels – Book 1

Flight of the Angels – Book 2

Path of the Angels – Book 3

Justice of the Angels – Book 4

Table of Contents

Introduction

Angels are a wonderful gift from GOD. **These stories are designed to be a bridge helping you to begin the biggest adventure in your life: Interacting with the Angels!** These twelve adventure stories let you accompany Dancing Wind, a teenage Native American Indian girl as she learns from a Lakota Indian Medicine man how to spirit track. Come along and travel with Dancing Wind as she encounters prospectors, priest, sheep herders, gamblers, a treacherous saloon keeper, a Apache and her flight for her life across the Sonoran Desert as she follows the guidance of her Guardian Angel.

The Guardian Angels in our life are a wonderful gift from GOD. **To those who do interact with their Guardian Angel; a world of wonder and delight can unfold in their life. Certainly my Guardian Angel has warned me of danger, had me rolling on the ground in laughter, as well as crying like Noah's flood.**

With an Angel at my side, Dancing Wind, Dan and I have had adventures I never envisioned possible. Follow Dancing Wind and her wise Lakota teacher as they encounter the spirits of priests, Indians, sheep herders, prospectors and treacherous enemies; and work with the Angels to take them *home*. I would hope that as you read these adventure stories you would open yourself to your Guardian Angel and allow them to show you their personal recognition signals for you. Each time you sit down to read these stories ask GOD to place a White Light of Protection around you and ask your Guardian Angel to sit beside you. As you begin your adventure with the Angels they may begin to communicate with you by causing you to vibrate, shake, tingle, cry, feel hot, or many other forms as they open the bridge to communicate with you. The very fortunate individuals may begin communicating directly with their Guardian Angel. Always ask GOD to surround you with a White Light of Protection and insist upon your Guardian Angels recognition signal when communicating with your Angel to be sure the information you receive is authentic.

I hope you enjoy these adventures with Guardian Angels and I sincerely hope that they help you connect with your own Guardian Angel. GOD Speed; and enjoy!

Angels are Love
Angels are Light
Angels are GOD's creatures of delight
They come to teach
They come to play
They come to help in delightful ways

Tracking Through Time

Dancing Wind was 15 years old. Her long, jet black hair that came from her mother's Arapaho Indian heritage and cool blue eyes identified her as a member of the Blue Star generation. She was a beautiful young woman who was intent on saving the world in her own special way. As a girl, Dancing Wind had spent much of her time learning the names of the native plants, their uses for healing or food, and where to find them. Her teacher was an old Indian she called Dan. He had long silver hair worn in braids, a brown leathery face, and a slow raspy voice that carried the tradition of oral history as a medal of honor.

Dan had taught Dancing Wind about nature and had helped her learn how to work with her Guardian Angel. He knew that she would one day learn to use her spiritual gifts and abilities to change the world for the better. The old teacher had already laid the groundwork by telling her the old stories of medicine men helping the lost spirits of men find their way home. He had taught her to track the trails of animals and men, and now he felt she was ready to learn more about the spirit world around her.

They set out on a sunny Saturday morning and arrived in the mountains south of the Pueblo of Abiquiu. Standing at a junction in the old dirt road near the rest stop and the picnic tables, they saw the road wind up into the mountains to the east. A canyon with a dry creek bed wound to the southwest. As Dancing Wind contemplated her two routes of travel, the morning sunrise begin to bring sunlight into the narrow canyon by the warm and the cold springs. Looking towards the south she saw a Spanish marker in the shape of an Angel revealed on the canyon wall. Her attention focused on the stone shadow Angel. The Angel was about one hundred and fifty feet tall and had one arm held up high and three fingers raised. The Angel was looking toward the narrow, seldom traveled canyon making an oath to GOD. Dancing Wind wondered what that promise was and if it would have any bearing on her adventures today. Dancing Winds Guardian Angel, with a crooked smile on one side of her mouth knew what lay beyond in the canyon, and she liked the lessons which were about to unfold.

★★Two hundred years earlier ★★

Nata was in a race she could not afford to lose. She was exhausted, and she could hear the sound of the horses, ridden by three Spanish slave traders, echoing on the rocks in the narrow canyon. If not for the love of her husband and young son she would have thrown herself in the river rather than run like a hunted animal into the mountains. She knew they were closing in, but she would never willingly be led away from her home to be traded as a slave. She knew that she could run faster if she did not have to carry her son, Ena, but she hated the thought of leaving him alone.

Ena was a good boy, and Nata knew he would obey any order she gave. Nata set him down in the tall green grass behind a large rock near the stream. She quickly told him to be still and silent until she returned. Ena was scared but he did not cry. Nata whispered her love and was gone as fast as a deer being chased by wolves. Her only hope was to reach the mountain called Sierra de Las Minas where her husband and brother worked as slaves in a Spanish gold mine.

Just about a mile past the warm and cold springs, ten miles south of Abiquiu, she was caught. The Spaniard deliberately slammed the horse he was riding into the skinny Indian girl, knocking her into the yellow flowered chamiso bushes along the creek. He was mad, and he intended to teach her a lesson she would never forget. The slave traders proceeded to rape and beat her with such brutality that before they were through she was dead. The three slave traders mounted their horses and rode away. Causing anguish and suffering was the way of these men. They would do many more evil deeds throughout their lives. They had no dignity, no honor, no sense of fair play and no respect for life.

No one has the right to hurt, violate or murder another. The nature spirits were so outraged at the violence and lack of remorse, that they withdrew the energy of the springs on the streams west branch and it dried up. The east branch of the stream that flows past the picnic tables is all that remains of the two stream branch's which flowed down through the canyon, and past Abiquiu.

The young woman's body lay lifeless on the ground. Because of the emotional stress, her spirit was lost. In spirit she replayed the end of her struggle. She tried to understand what she did wrong, but she simply could not get past the fear and the anguish she felt in the last horrible moments of her life. As the seasons passed and the years went by she relived those last moments time and again.

★★Two hundred years later★★

She was in no hurry today so Dancing Wind took the trail less traveled, and Dan followed along behind her as she took a canyon going to the southwest towards the mountain she had heard the wind call "Sierra de las Minas." Dan, the old Indian who is teaching the teenager to track, had often told her: *"A trail is never tracked by accident. For every trail that you choose to follow, there is a reason."*

As she followed the Spanish Trail to the southwest towards Sierra de las Minas, off in the distance about four hundred yards up into the dry canyon, Dancing Wind saw the little baby boy Ena hidden in the grass and Chamiso bushes. So Dancing Wind stopped to talk to the little Indian boy's spirit. The baby's story moved Dancing Wind to uncontrollable tears as the infant described the men chasing his mother and how he was waiting here for her return. The little boy had been waiting for his mother for two centuries, and she had not returned for him! The infant told Dancing Wind that he was very worried about his mother as three bad men had been chasing her.

Dancing Wind took the Spirit into her arms and gave him hugs and kisses and all the love she could pour out of her heart. Then Dancing Wind's Guardian Angel who had been witnessing the unfolding events whispered into Dancing Wind's ear: *"Ask the little boy if he will take you to his mother"* and so Dancing Wind followed the Angel's advice. Hand in hand, Dancing Wind, the little Indian boy Ena's spirit, and both of their Guardian Angels traveled up the canyon approximately a mile Dan followed along behind Dancing Wind and Ena. Dan was very happy with the way today's lessons were unfolding. Dan knew that Dancing Wind would never forget the lessons she was learning today.

When the little boy saw his mother's spirit he let go of Dancing Wind's hand and in a wild rush jumped into his mother's arms. The mother and son were reunited after more than two centuries apart! Everyone was in tears. They were happy and sorrowful at the same time. The tears flowed down Dancing Wind's cheeks; she was overjoyed with the reunion, yet she was outraged at what the Spaniards had done to Nata.

Dancing Wind had literally seen, felt, and experienced all that Nata had endured at the hands of her attackers. Now she was overjoyed that she could reunite the mother with her child. Never had Dancing Wind felt such emotions of both outrage and sorrow for what had happened. At the same time she was so happy that she could bring the lost little boy's spirit back to his mother's spirit so that they could be reunited again after so many years apart!

Dancing Wind then told Nata and her son Ena that if they wanted to go *home* next weekend that she would return to the grassy meadow near where she found her son and help them both go *home*. She just asked them to also pass the word on to the other spirits that they knew that she would also be happy to help any spirits who wanted help returning *home* when she returned to the meadow near the mouth of the canyon.

★★★★

Dancing Wind returned back down the narrow canyon to where she had found the baby boy because she had seen several more spirits there. On the west side of the canyon she had seen another spirit, so she started talking softly and lovingly coaxing and encouraging him to come out of his hiding spot among the rocks. He too had come from Abiquiu years earlier, fleeing into these mountains for shelter from the men who wrongly accused him of a bad crime. Even though he was completely innocent of the crime, angry men incited by the guilty parties who had actually committed the crime, blamed him. The guilty parties accused the innocent man and pointed out his fear and nervousness when the group of angry men confronted him. The people who knew he was innocent of the crime accused him so suspicion would not fall upon them.

The innocent man fled to try and save his life from the angry crowd which pursued him. When the angry mob of men caught up with the innocent man they promptly murdered the man in the same canyon just across from where the little baby boy Ena's spirit watched! Dancing Wind saw the events unfold in front of her as the spirit showed her pictures of what he experienced. Dancing Wind saw his murder in such detail that she even saw where the murder weapon was thrown after the angry mob murdered him. She understood the rage he felt of being wrongly accused of a crime he had nothing to do with. She felt his pain and fear as the mob attacked him and murdered this innocent man. She prayed to GOD and the Angels for him. She told him to let go of his fear, let go of his pain, let go of his anger, and if he was willing to go *home* she would help him do so. She prayed to GOD and his Angels to surround the injured spirit with love and forgiveness. She told him she would be back this coming weekend at the meadow just within his sight, to the north, to help him go *home* should he choose to do so. Then she also asked him to pass the word on to any other spirits that he might encounter who also wished to go *home*.

Nearby, Dancing Wind also saw the spirit of a man who liked to drink beer. While drunk, he had an auto accident and drove off the road into the canyon where he died. He was sitting beside his old wrecked car which he had destroyed in his car accident. Being here in spirit was like being in hell for him, there was not a cold beer anywhere and he wanted a beer desperately!

When Dancing Wind talked to the man who liked to drink beer about going *home* he was not too interested in that, what he wanted most was a beer! Dancing Wind told him that if he wanted to go *home* next weekend, she would come and help him if he wanted to. Then Dancing Wind described how the Door of Light would appear with one Angel on each side of the door.

The man who liked to drink beer told Dancing Wind, "You're full of shit. I don't need your help."

Dancing Wind replied: "I will be in that meadow should you choose to come, and I would appreciate it if you would please pass the word around." So Dancing Wind spent her day helping the spirits who had come to die within and near the narrow canyon on the way to Sierra de las Minas and did not know how to find their way *home*.

★★★★

A week passed quickly and as promised Dancing Wind returned to the small meadow in the narrow canyon near where she first encountered Ena's spirit. The little Indian boy's spirit ran from his mother's side and gave Dancing Wind a big hug. Then he went over to Dan who was teaching Dancing Wind how to track in the spirit realm, and spoke with him. He grabbed hold of Dan's left hand and squeezed it to ensure he had Dan's full attention. While holding Dan's hand, the little Indian talked about how he wanted to spend more time with Dan. He wanted to be as wise as Dan was, and though he was going *home* now with his mother, he hoped to return shortly as a child of someone Dan held very dear to his heart. Dan was so touched by the little spirit's love and desire that it touched Dan's heart and caused tears to stream down his weathered face as he listened to the little boy pour out his love and respect for the old teacher.

Dancing Wind then asked GOD and his Angels for help and guidance. Then she asked GOD to place a white light of protection around Dan and her and all the spirits assembled her in love and light. Next she lit incense in a large circle around the meadow. Slowly Dancing Wind began moving around the outside of the large circle of incense while she beat on her small hand drum that Dan had made for her. As she walked, she began drumming very slowly allowing lots of time for the spirits to join her in the circle as she drummed. Then gradually she beat the drum faster and faster. One after another the Indian and Spanish spirits fell in behind her following her around the circle.

The Wind Spirits came and blew their wind around the circle to add their helpful energy. As the pace picked up faster and faster, every spirit who chose to go *home* was moving through the circle. Suddenly a door filled with light opened up with two Angels standing guard; one on each side of the Door of Light. The procession of Indians traveled into the Door of Light between the two Angels. Suddenly out from the piñon trees, where he had been hiding and watching, rushed the man who liked beer and had told Dancing Wind that she was "full of shit". He came running as fast as he could, clamoring to get into the line because he did not want to be left behind! When the last spirit had gone *home* the door disappeared as suddenly as it had appeared. As the two Angels returned to Heaven with GOD, the wind suddenly ceased blowing. All was quiet in the meadow. Thirty eight Indian and Hispanic spirits had gone *home*! For Dancing Wind it was really the beginning of her adventures, for this was the first time she had successfully tracked numerous spirits through time and space and been able to give them the individual help and attention they needed so that they could return *home*.

Some people look for
Treasures in the mountains
Some people look for
Treasure in the hills
But the greatest treasure of all
Is a heart that Love fills

The Treasure of Francisco Martinez

Two older men heard a story about a young teenage girl who could talk to Angels and track trails going through the mountains that were centuries old. So, they went to find the teenager in the small village of Abiquiu where the painter Georgia O'Keeffe was inspired to create some of her famous paintings.

There, in a small older trailer, they met the teenager and asked her to accompany them into the mountains to the northeast of Dixon. They told her that on a specific mountain to the northeast of Dixon there is a ghost who guards the money he has buried long ago.

They know this because several years ago three men climbed the mountain to dig up his treasure, only to flee when the ghost suddenly appeared out of nowhere and chased them off his mountain. Dancing Wind told them to come back the following weekend, and she would accompany them into the mountains and check out their story. When the weekend came, they picked up Dancing Wind in their truck and took her up into the mountains.

Once they were up in the mountains the men decided to test the teenage girl by asking which of the mountains the ghost was on. They wanted to see if she could pick the right mountain. It only took her an instant to see the ghost, and for her to identify the mountain where he guarded his treasure. Then the two men waited by the truck for Dancing Wind to go up the mountain to get the treasure.

When she reached the top of the mountain, Dancing Wind approached the ghost and asked him his name. He told her as they sat down to talk that his name was Francisco Martinez and he was a sheepherder and later on a landowner. He also stated that he was tired of people coming here trying to steal his money! Because Dancing Wind is a forward and honest teenager, she simply told the truth to Francisco; she was here looking for his money! Francisco told Dancing Wind he did not want anyone to steal his money, but if she earned it she would not be stealing it! What Francisco told Dancing Wind was that if she would find his girlfriend Angelina Ramirez and give her half the money then Francisco would give her the other half. So with the challenge of having to find Francisco's girlfriend, they parted ways with Dancing Wind climbing down the mountain, while Francisco staying on the mountain top.

At the bottom of the mountain the two men waited by their truck for the teenager to bring them the money. When she told them that she would have to work for the money by finding Francisco's girlfriend and giving her half the money they were both disgusted at the thought of further work, as well as Dancing Winds failure to bring them the treasure. As Dancing Wind removed her back pack in which she carried her water and set it on the hood of the truck one of the two men casually walked over to her backpack and lifted it up and peaked inside to satisfy himself that she was not hiding the treasure in her back pack and keeping it all for herself.

That evening the two men drove Dancing Wind back home to Abiquiu. To themselves they said it does no good to talk to ghost if they will not hand over their treasure. Certainly that trip had been a waste of time. Never again did they go to the mountain with Dancing Wind.

When Dancing Wind got home, she decided to consult with her mentor, Dan, an old Lakota Indian, who was teaching her how to track old trails. Dan told her to go to the courthouse and check the tax records, and landowner plates to see if Dancing Wind could find any records about Francisco Martinez, because he wanted her to learn to balance her approach to tracking between the spirit world and the physical world. When Dancing Wind searched the Espanola tax records she found the plate of Francisco's land, in the village of Dixon, dated 1920. These documents supported her conversation with the spirit that he owned land and lived in the time frame he said.

In her discussions with Francisco Martinez on subsequent weekends, Dancing Wind learned more about Francisco. He told her he was born in 1870 and went into spirit in 1930. He told her about the tall grass that used to be on the mountains and the numerous deer herds. Francisco told her how he would hunt the deer with a .22 rifle. He talked about the sheep he watched over, and he would show Dancing Wind as they walked through the woods where he camped and often had picnics with his girlfriend Angelina. At one place, he showed Dancing Wind where his cast iron frying pan was located. Surprisingly, to Dancing Wind the old cast iron frying pan was much thinner than today's modern cast iron cookware.

Dancing Wind came to realize that Francisco's girlfriend was also in spirit and she stayed around Francisco, but since Francisco could not accept the fact she was in spirit, he refused to see her. When Dancing Wind helped Francisco to see that his girlfriend was right there beside him, instead of being happy, Francisco was unhappy and sullen as he felt he had been cheated by Dancing Wind, who really just wanted to steal his money so he refused to pay Dancing Wind anything!

When dealing with people or spirits there has to be dignity, honor, fair play, and trust.

It's a two way street that must go both ways! It is never the letter of the agreement, which is important; it is the spirit of the agreement that has to be met!

Now came the hard part for Dancing Wind, fulfilling the spirit of the agreement. At Dan's suggestion, Dancing Wind began a process of learning what Francisco Martinez really wanted. Dancing Wind would sit down in a dry arroyo and talk with Francisco and Angelina. In their discussions, she learned that what they really wanted was to be married to each other.

★★★★

On a weekend that Dancing Wind did not go up to see Francisco and Angelina, dawn found her tracking on the Old Spanish Trail along the Chama River with her teacher Dan. As they tracked along the Old Spanish Trail they stopped to discuss the ecology of the area. Long ago the area now covered by the Abiquiu dam was once a grass land with tall grass and herds of elk grazed there. Dan commented to Dancing Wind, that the trees were very sad about the abuse of the environment.

Dancing Wind asked Dan, "Can you teach me how to talk to the trees? "

Dan told her to park the jeep. They both got out and walked over and sat beneath a Juniper tree. Then Dan sat under the tree and instructed Dancing Wind to be sure she was touching the tree. So Dancing Wind sat under the tree with her back against the main tree trunk.

Then Dan and Dancing Wind said prayers to the *Spirit whom moves through all things (GOD)*. They prayed for the environment, they prayed for the animals who lived there, they prayed to Mother Earth and they prayed that man would open his eyes and begin to learn to cherish and protect the Mother Earth. Then they prayed that they might be able to have clear communication with the tree they sat under.

The tree expressed to Dan and Dancing Wind how hard it was without sufficient water. It expressed its desire to help the environment. It despaired over the way people treated the environment. It was doing its best to help but it was a hard struggle. He had been badly hurt when a man cut off one of his branches. The tree indicated it was dying now because the injury had allowed bugs to enter it and they were slowly killing the tree. Tears were running down Dancing Winds face as she had been so moved her spirit encounter with the tree.

Getting up from the tree she noticed the limb of the tree which had been cut off. Dancing Wind turned to Dan and said, "Wait here, I'll be back." Then she walked to her jeep and got her canteen of water and carefully poured out the water and the base of the tree giving it her water.

Then as they got up to leave, Dan told her, "Just wait here as I see we have company." Dan approached them first as he wanted to understand what spirit form had come in to watch them beside the tree. As the Lakota Indian approached the three spirits he realized that they were enlightened spirits who in their last life were priest.

★★★★

The Old Spanish Trail ran from Santa Fe, New Mexico all the way west to Los Angeles, California. There, on the Old Spanish Trail she met the spirits of three German priests. In the 1700's, the German priest were caught by a Comanche war party that was out raiding. While the priest had rifles and the ability to fight off the war party, they refused to use their rifles to fire on the Indians and take human life. These priests were very enlightened and held all life as sacred.

★★★★

The Comanche war party was not so enlightened and did not hold their enemies' lives as sacred. The Comanche thought all individuals not of their tribe were enemies. The war party tortured the priests until they died then stole their belongings. Dancing Wind asked the spirits if she could do anything for them or to help them in any way. They asked her to say a prayer for them in the mission at Abiquiu, and light three candles in the mission for them.

Two weeks later, she purchased the candles and took them to the altar of the Abiquiu mission. She set the candles on a metal tray so they could not accidentally cause a fire in the old mission. Then she lit all three candles then she called the three German priests into the church, to show them she was honoring her promise to light the three candles in the Abiquiu church for them.

From her heart she poured out her request to GOD that he watch over and help the three good priests and fill them to over flowing with his love and light, as she said the best prayer for them that she could. As the words flowed from her heart, Dancing Wind asked GOD to send his Angels to surround the three holy men with his love and light, and all the peace and unity that their hearts could hold. She asked the Angels to watch over these good men and help them in their work (since their death centuries earlier they were doing their best to help keep the environment in balance and they were working with Mother Earth and the Nature Spirits). She poured out her heart to GOD to relieve the priest of any pain from their injuries and fill them with Mother Mary's divine love. Before Dancing Wind even got to the part of her prayer where she asked GOD to fill the priest with Dignity, Honor and Integrity and help them in their work, she could feel the presence of many Angels filling the church and the hearts of the three priests with their overflowing love. Before leaving, Dancing Wind knew that making the effort to keep her promise to the German priests resulted in her making three very good friends.

As Dancing Wind got up to leave the Abiquiu mission Lily her Guardian Angel said, *"You did that nicely. Since you have gotten the priest to travel from the site of their death, you have increased the likely hood that in the future you will be able to take them home. What I would like you to do is continue the dialogue with them. You might be happily surprised at the good which may result."*

★★★★

The following weekend Dancing Wind returned to talk to Francisco and Angelina as she wanted to ensure she did everything they wanted for their wedding. She wanted to make sure she knew everything that was important to them to insure that she properly fulfilled the spirit of the agreement she had with Francisco. When she asked them if they wanted roses, they asked: "Why would we want roses? "Roses were not important to them. But Dancing Wind's questions prompted them to put pictures into her head showing her exactly what they wanted. Francisco's pictures showed Dancing Wind that in their day the bride and groom got married walking together holding hands with a rosary in their hands with the cross hanging down from between there joined hands. They also wanted three candles. Two candles were to be lit on each Sunday for the two weeks prior to the wedding, the third candle was to be lit at the wedding on the third Sunday night. So, each Sunday prior to the wedding, Dancing Wind would call in the spirits of Francisco and Angelina and show them she was honoring their request by lighting a candle for them.

★★★★

On the weekend that Dancing Wind was traveling north into the mountains for the marriage of Francisco to Angelina, she stopped and invited the spirits of the German priests to accompany her to the wedding. It was a nice surprise when the German priests accepted Dancing Wind's invitation and jumped into the car with her!

At the wedding Dancing Wind surprised Angelina with the rosary she had promised to bring. She also brought a small chocolate wedding cake, bottled water, and a CD player to provide the music for the wedding.

They had a wedding ceremony complete with music, cake, and water. The guests as well as the Wind Spirits, who decided to attend the ceremony, were dancing all about enjoying the music. Dancing Wind had to ask the Wind Spirits to calm down to enable her to light the third candle and to allow the candle to remain lit. The Wind Spirits honored her request.

After the wedding was completed and Francisco and Angelina Martinez were married, Dancing Wind asked the married couple what to do with the cake, and they said to leave it here on the ground next to the trees and this stream along with the water bottles. Instantly, both of the bottles of water fell over. Angelina then said a prayer to GOD and the Water Spirits that the stream in the dry arroyo would flow again as it did in the old days. Angelina then had Dancing Wind place the Rosary under a rock in the dry arroyo. Dancing Wind told Francisco, Angelina, and all the wedding guests that had come to the wedding party, that in two weeks she would return and help all who chose to go *home*. She asked all present to inform any spirit they were aware of to come as well. She would assist any spirit wanting help return *home*.

Francisco told her he was happy she had brought the priests with her to his wedding, as priest at the weddings were not very common. He told her that the three priests and the chocolate cake were nice surprises. That Sunday night Dancing Wind lit a third candle (the one lit at the wedding and blown out by the Wind Spirits) and called in Francisco and Angelina Martinez and let them know that she had kept the letter of the agreement and more importantly the spirit of the agreement. She asked Francisco to honor his part of the agreement when she returned next week.

When Dancing Wind returned to the mountain to see Francisco a week later, she brought with her a bag of food for a coyote that she had seen near where Francisco and Angelina sat watching over the mountainside below. She could not find Francisco or Angelina but she took the time to feed the skinny coyote as one must show compassion and care towards all of Mother Nature's animals. Then Dancing Wind returned home to Abiquiu.

The following weekend arrived quickly and Dancing Wind went to the arroyo on the mountain where she had told the spirits she would meet them to help all the spirits who wanted to return *home*. The arroyo that had been dry at the time of the wedding now had water flowing around the stone under which Angelina Martinez had directed Dancing Wind to place the rosary when she asked GOD and the Water Spirits for their blessing. For literally the action of prayer to GOD coupled with the action the Spirit had requested of Dancing Wind resulted in the water now flowing in what had been a dry arroyo.

Lily told Dancing Wind, "*It is very important to keep your word with the spirits as the word gets around and travels far and wide if you are a spirit who keeps your word or not. The reputation you want is for honesty and integrity.*" By word of mouth the Spirits will know if you will keep your word to them or not. One ghost may have heard about you from another ghost or spirit hundreds of miles away. Lily added, "*It is not unusual for one ghost, should the ghost chose to know, about other ghost or even the trails that you are tracking or will be tracking in the future even if these locations are hundreds of miles apart!*

As the spirits started arriving, Dancing Wind went to turn on her portable CD player to play soothing flute music. She wanted to relax the numerous spirits whom had gathered around her and gradually build up the energy before calling in the Angels, but her batteries were dead! So Dancing Wind picked up a tin can to drum on and started drumming and walking in a circle as the spirits of Indian men, women, and children joined in behind her. The three German priests joined in too as they sang and drummed on three spirit drums they had created by thought. Faster and faster the energy built up until suddenly a door filled with light appeared, on the edge of the circle the spirits were dancing around. On each side of the door filled with light stood an Angel guarding the door. The spirits shot through the door going *home* to GOD. The Angels were gone as suddenly as they had appeared and the door closed behind them.

About a dozen spirits had chosen to go *home,* and they did so. Angelina and Francisco chose to stay on their mountain. They are still there now. Lily told Dancing Wind, "Possibly Angelina will go *home* if she is unable to convince Francisco to go with her. If this were to happen, Francisco is faced with his decision; is it love or money he choose to make the top priority of his existence? If he chooses to make money, he and Angelina will be tied to the mountain forever. If he chooses love both of them will be able to go *home.* In your own life as well you must constantly ask yourself which you value most. The decision YOU make then determines the path you will follow."

Francisco told Dancing Wind to return with a shovel the next time she returned. In the spirit of a helping nature, and to surprise Francisco and Angelina; when Dancing Wind returned the following weekend, she also brought along dry land grass seed, a salt block, and a deer feed block to help the deer whom lived up on the mountain.

Instead of fulfilling the gift Francisco promised, he had Dancing Wind dig holes in the ground covered in patches of snow, and plant the grass seed. He showed her where to place the salt block and the deer feed block. Francisco made no effort to show Dancing Wind the money he promised.

The four deer were keeping an eye on Dancing Wind. They did not come in close but instead sent their spirits to keep an eye on her. These four deer knew it was much safer to use their spirit's instead of their physical bodies to observe humans. Often times humans tried to kill them.

The deer observed the planting of the grass seed and the placing of the deer feed block and the salt block. These four deer were the last of the large herds that roamed these mountains for centuries and had been wiped out by the destruction of the grass that the deer depended on for their food. The loss of the grass due to overgrazing by sheep and heavy hunting killed hundreds of deer. The deer's spirits showed Dancing Wind that because of her actions a new fawn would be born in the spring. The way the deer communicated with Dancing Wind and with each other is by visualizing what they want to communicate. The deer put pictures of what they wish to say in their mind then open their mind up for the animal, spirit or person to see. When Dancing Wind "spoke" with the deer, she did the same thing; put pictures in her mind of what she wanted to say to the deer. That is how animals communicate or people can talk to animals. Francisco and Angelina then sat on a rock together and discussed the gift that Dancing Wind would receive the next time she returned as well as how their share was to be used.

★★★★

Dancing Wind arrived on the mountain on a snowy winter's day for Francisco to show her where his money was hidden. Snow clouds were moving in, blocking more and more of mountains from view and covering them with snow. Dancing Wind then asked the Snow Pixies if they would hold off making snow on this mountain until she had a chance to finish her work. The Snow Pixies told her they would give her the time she needed.

★★★★

With heavy snow falling on the adjoining mountains but not theirs, Dancing Wind followed Francisco up into the mountains to a saddle of the skyline, he told her to dig and she would find the gift he had for her. As Dancing Wind dug down into the frozen ground he told her to go deeper and to be careful not to hit the box with her digging tools. She dug deeper and deeper, to exhaustion, in her effort until she hit bedrock and could go no deeper.

Francisco had deliberately lied to Dancing Wind! The hole filled with Dancing Wind's tears as they ran down her cheeks into the empty hole. Even in the end, Dancing Wind showed honor and respect, taking out a paper bag of sacred corn and planting it in Mother Earth's soil so it would grow in the spring. Where Dancing Wind had shown dignity, honor, fair play, and respect, Francisco Martinez chose not to honor her with the same dignity, honor, fair play and respect she had shown him!

As Dancing Wind walked across the mountains toward the car, the Snow Pixies brought snow to the mountain. Soon everything was covered in white. The snow covered the ground and her car, hiding them in a blanket of white snow, but it could not cover the tears running down her face nor hide her broken heart!

When you give the homeless a helping hand
Love is like a rainbow
Not prejudice to any race
Love is like a rainbow
Bringing a smile to GOD's face

The Apache

On the western edge of the Malpais (a Spanish word meaning Bad Lands; which is an accurate description of the fields of sharp jagged black lava rocks) lives the spirit of an Apache warrior. He had heard stories from other spirits of living people who could talk to spirits and help spirits go home. He found out the names of two of these people were Dancing Wind and Dan. Dan is an old Lakota Indian who has taken Dancing Wind under his wing to teach her how to track and help spirits go *home*. With this information, the Apache traveled hundreds of miles across the American southwest desert to the houses of each of the trackers to ask for their help.

The Apache could have walked if he chose to do so; but spirits can also travel hundreds of miles in the blink of an eye. Just by thinking where they want to be, a spirit can instantly transport themselves to the location or place that they are thinking about. This is a gift of the Spirit realm that may be used by Angels and earthbound spirits. Since the Apache warrior had made the effort to contact Dancing Wind and Dan, they agreed to travel to his area to help him.

One hundred and fifty years ago, the Apaches' main food sources were the wild game they hunted and the plants that were gathered from the wild. Often they traveled hundreds of miles locating food in the desert southwest. They had their favorite hunting areas for each season. Some of the wild game animals which were major food sources for the Apaches included antelope, bison, elk, deer, javelinas, turkeys, rabbits, and snakes. They would also supplement the meat with plants that they harvested from Mother Earth such as piñon (pine) and oak nuts in the fall, currants, and cattail and bull rush roots. Juniper berries were cut open then dried. Larger seeds like amaranth and grass, sotol, and century plant were baked over hot coals to become edible. The Apaches used over two hundred plants and animals as food sources. Since they were nomadic "hunter gathers" they tended to travel in small bands or family units. Food was often in short supply, and they traveled hundreds of miles to their favorite locations in search of food. Had they traveled in larger groups, feeding the whole tribe would have been impossible.

This was the environment that the Apache lived in when the Spanish and white man invaded their hunting grounds. The invaders brought cattle and sheep as well as large numbers of people. The cattle and sheep overgrazed the grasslands that had supported wild game, while the invaders hunted what game was left using modern rifles. Almost nothing was left for the Apache, no matter how far they roamed.

★★★★

If the Apache hunted the cattle or sheep which were displacing their wild game then the Spanish and Anglos hunted down the Indians and killed them, justifying it as payback for stealing their livestock. The last massacre of Apaches occurred in about 1929 while Apaches were killing some cattle for the meat they needed to get them through the winter. Francisco Fimbres had driven a small herd of cattle back into the mountains on border of New Mexico and Arizona, a little north of our border with Mexico. The cattle were placed there as bait to induce the Apaches to come into the trap he created. Hidden nearby was a group of men laying in ambush. Then the Apaches were killed when they came into the trap. Francisco Fimbres was not charged with murder for killing these Apaches. After all, it was a common saying: "The only good Indian is a dead Indian."

★★1850's★★

It was in these times that the Apache left his hungry wife and son and took off to find food for his family and himself. Over a century ago, the Apache had told his wife and son that they were to remain where they were and not go anywhere as he would be back for them as soon as he could. He left his family in a small grassy clearing on the west side of the Malpais near the lava tubes and took off hunting for food. He knew that this clearing was safe from the invaders because when he went on war parties with other Apache warriors, this is where they always went to hide after the raid. He told his wife and son to remain in this safe place and not go anywhere until he returned with some food.

On this hunt, the Apache came across a group of seven mules. His family was saved! He saw the seven mules as transportation for himself and his family and as they got hungry, each mule could be butchered to provide hundreds of pounds of meat. Apaches really enjoyed eating mules. All he had to do was steal the mules and return to his family. What he did not count on was the owner of the mules seeing him gather the mules and start to ride off with them.

As the Apache was riding off with the stolen mules, the mules' owner had a clear shot at the Apache with his rifle. He took it and killed him! The man, who killed the Apache, saw it simply as a lucky break.

To catch a thief in the act of stealing his mules and be fortunate enough to kill the thief, made him very happy. Often people do not realize the consequences of their actions, and often there are far reaching consequences!

Back in the Malpais, the Apache's wife and infant son waited for his return. She was an honorable woman and so she honored her husband's request that she wait in the grassy clearing for his return. With her son at her side, she waited until they both starved to death. To this day, her spirit is still there with her infant son beside her, waiting for her husband to return!

★★Present day★★

One day when Dancing Wind was meeting with Dan at his house they were discussing the visits by the Apache spirit. Then suddenly to their surprise the Apache spirit appeared before them both. The Apache told Dancing Wind and Dan that he had buried gold and silver in the Malpais in a small kidney bean shaped island of grass surrounded by high walls of lava located in the lava fields south of Grants. This was a safe shelter where they could remain hidden from the Whites and Mexicans who wished to kill them. This gold and silver had come from ambushing a Spanish pack train hauling gold and silver to Mexico and from some outlaws the Apaches had taken the gold from. The Apache went into detail about these gold and silver caches.

The way the Apache warrior communicated with Dancing Wind and her Indian teacher Dan was by picturing or envisioning in his mind what he was saying. Then Dancing Wind and Dan would see these pictures in their mind. The Apache showed Dancing Wind and Dan two treasures he had placed in the hideout. Both treasures were on the east side of their hideout up against the Malpais walls. The north most treasure consisted of gold and silver coins taken from outlaws and this money was in a saddle bag. This first treasure was not buried very deep as it was hidden by the Apache warrior talking to Dancing Wind and Dan. The second treasure was also on the east side of the small grassy park. This treasure was buried much deeper as it was hidden by an Apache war party which included the Apache warrior telling the story. This second treasure was taken from a Spanish pack train headed past the Malpais going to Mexico.

The Spanish men did not survive the ambush by the Apache war party which occurred in the early 1800's. The war party took the gold and silver bars of bullion and then hid them in their hide out by caving in the walls and throwing many lava rocks on top of the cache of gold and silver bars still in the panniers (leather bags) used to transport the treasure.

The Apache told both Dancing Wind and Dan that, "You can take the right hand or the south most treasure, which was obtained from the Spanish pack train. The left hand, or north most treasure is not to be touched by you." The Apache also told them not to electronically scan the left or north most site. He told them, "You are to locate the southern deposit by spirit and by looking, following the directions he had given them.

"Be careful though as there here are four Apache's presently guarding the site. They have been taught to kill intruders. They come by the site whenever they have a little free time they drive on by. If one of them should see your vehicle parked near this site you can expect all four of them will arrive within an hour."

The Apache went on to say, "It is because of these two Apache who do not believe what you say that you will let them see for themselves what spirit has told you. "You shall tell the Apaches guarding the site that THE SPIRIT THAT MOVES THROUGH ALL THINGS is changing their job to a more important job, a more important need. You shall say to them that the Apaches *are to no longer guard this site and that IT IS ENOUGH TO HOLD THIS GROUND AS SACRED IN THEIR HEARTS. What the Spirit needs is far more important, it needs for everyone to place in the sacred ground of Mother Earth plants and seeds. It is especially important to plant edible plants and fruit trees at all the springs, water holes, streams, and shelters that they know of. You shall take a best friend or a child with you. Show them how to plant the edible plant or fruit tree and care for the land. It is time to give back to Mother Earth! Do not always take from Mother Earth. Do not take your food on the table for granted for it will not always be there! You must plant lots of fruit trees, asparagus plants, raspberries, blackberries, mulberries, Nanking cherries, pumpkins, corn, squash and native dry land grasses for the horses.*

"When you talk to the Apaches, two of the four will not believe you. These two should be taken to the left or north cache and told to dig it up. You must ask them what is there, but they will not know! Then tell them that the Spirit has told you that there are gold and silver coins in the leather saddle bags. You are to tell them that all four of you Apaches are to: Only take what you need—not more— but you are to come as often as your Spirit wants and calls you to.

"Have a child on the reservation who is good with computers to arrange the sale—one coin at a time—on the computer. In other words, with a digital picture at an auction site like E-Bay. This will give you the cash you need. This money should only be used for three things:

1. Edible plants / grass you plant everywhere you know that there is water.
2. Food for the trip
3. Gas for the trip

Use this money wisely, as if I am watching you! For I will be watching you!
"A time of Earth changes and starvation will come upon the land shortly. You must prepare for it NOW! I do not want your family to starve to death as my family did!

Beginning now, plant the edible plants and fruit trees everywhere you know. Do it NOW! Do it like your lives depend on it! For your lives and our people's lives depend on your taking action now! Do not depend on government rations; soon they will be gone!

The Apache told Dancing Wind and Dan that they could have one of the two deposits if they helped his wife and daughter go *home* with him. The Apache showed them that his wife and son were on the south end of this hideout. They were now earthbound spirits. The Apache's young wife and son are still there in the Malpais waiting for her husband to return and bring them food and water! She and her son still wait as they have waited over a hundred years while they died of starvation!

When Dancing Wind encountered the earthbound spirits of infant boy and her mother, tears of sorrow and sympathy flowed down Dancing Wind's face as she actually felt the hunger, the thirst, and the overwhelming despair the woman felt while waiting for her husband. Dan showed Dancing Wind how to give them both food and water, by sincerely and lovingly thinking and visualizing that action. Dancing Wind gave the spirits of the Apache's wife and child food and water and told them she would return and take them *home*. When she traveled to the Malpais, she expected the husband to guide her to his wife and son so she could help them. Dancing Wind's heart was so moved when she saw the little infant with the black hair and the brown eyes. To Dancing Wind the little boy's brown eyes actually showed blue with an advanced spiritual understanding. Dancing Wind's Guardian Angel told her the little boy had the ability to return *home,* but he would not use his ability to go *home* as he realized his mother needed him. He felt the best way to help his mother was to stay at her side, until he could help her go *home,* together with him.

Then Dancing Wind told the Apache, his wife, and infant son that she would travel to the Malpais and when she did so, she would bring them some sun dried jerky, water, biscuits, and jam. So not only was Dancing Wind showing positive, loving thoughts but she was following up thoughts with positive loving action, literally traveling hundreds of miles and taking food to them. Then they both planned a trip out to the Malpais to meet the Apache on his home ground to let him lead them to his wife and daughter. Then Dancing Wind would try and help all three earthbound spirits go *home*.

A key element to working as a Spirit Tracker is to show other spirits dignity, honor, peace and unity. In short, you try and live by the Golden Rule. Treat others like you would like to be treated. You choose the spirit trails you track. Spirit tracking is a learning experience and no trail is ever tracked by accident! If you choose to track a trail, with it comes an obligation to do your best to help the spirits you encounter when possible. It is always nice to track a trail hoping or expecting to make a recovery of a small cache of gold or silver coins; but most spirits can only give you love or a thank you. You must help these spirits too; it is part of one's spiritual obligation or spiritual path.

Yet there are times when a Spirit does not, or will not, show you the same integrity, dignity, honor, peace and unity that you show them, and then it is best to walk away. Just as some people are not very nice, some spirits are not very nice; it is best to just wash your hands of them—just walk away! Such was the case with the Apache; he would not show Dancing Wind nor Dan the same integrity, dignity, honor, peace and unity they had shown him and his family. He had asked them for their help and when they came to help; the Apache warrior treacherously attacked them both numerous times by trying to forcefully enter their body and take possession and control of them. This Dan and Dancing Wind would NEVER allow. By firmly holding a white light of protection around themselves the Apache could not forcefully gain entrance into their bodies. Repeatedly the Apache would come rushing in at them trying to force his way into their physical body, yet the assaults were futile. As they offered to work with him, instead the Apache would try and force his way into their bodies coming up from the ground, down from above and rushing their backs as he neither intended to work with them and instead The Apache felt treachery was the most effective approach so he kept trying to force his way into them.

All the Apaches treacherous attacks did was make Dan and Dancing Wind angry. Had the Apache accepted their help he could have been reunited with his family and accompanied them *home*. Dancing Wind realized the Apache had lied to her about his intentions. He wanted to take control of her body. As Dan and Dancing Wind prepared to leave the Malpais Dancing Wind did keep her word, she left jerky (dried meat), water, biscuits and jam by the western edge of the Malpais for the Apache's family— then left!

★★★★

Should you be driving past the Malpais or other hostile terrain where you would not want to be stranded, please say a prayer to GOD. Ask him to send his Angels to help the lost spirits and individuals to find their way *home* to GOD's all encompassing love. It may be your lost father, mother, sister, brother or your child who needs your prayers. Believe me, GOD hears your prayers!

Love
Love in the Morning
Love in the Night
Helps all GOD's Children
To sleep tight

The Watering Hole Saloon

Molly O' Brian and Dancing Wind were having a woman's day out. Both women were going out for a drive and then they planned to end the day in Santa Fe at the T-Bone Steak House, on the south end of town. Molly was letting her red hair fly in the wind and pushing her jeep wrangler for all it was worth on the dirt road. She was driving as fast as she could and still keep the jeep on the old dirt road. She occasionally swerved to avoid the deepest pot holes. Dancing Wind was laying back in her seat with her feet propped up on the dash, her eyes closed, and just enjoying the sun on her face, and the wind blowing her long black hair while enjoying her dear friend's company. Molly O'Brien was also relaxing in her way, pushing the jeep as fast as she could, yet just barely keeping it on the road and out of the bar ditches.

The hours passed as they drove through America's Southwest desert, when in the distance Molly first noticed a patch of green. As they drove closer; the green patch became a small watering hole with several old cottonwood trees growing there. Some of the trees looked dead but judging from their size they must have been well over a hundred years old, some of the old trees were just barely hanging on to life. There were younger trees growing up, which would in time replace the old dead cottonwood trees.

As the jeep approached the water hole and the cottonwoods, Molly O'Brien hit the brakes so abruptly the jeep wrangler went into a skid. Dancing Wind was thrown forward, and felt the seat belt restrain her forward movement. If she was not awake before she was certainly awake now! First Dancing Wind looked around to see a physical reason that Molly had so abruptly slammed on the brakes. When she saw nothing nearby, Dancing Wind scanned the surrounding terrain. Dancing Wind squinted through the cloud of dust that had engulfed the women after hitting the brakes, but she did not see any physical danger, or anything but desert all around them. Dancing Wind looked inquiringly at Molly. She noticed Molly's attention focused on the ruins or foundation of where a building used to be.

Slowly Dancing Wind began picking up the presence of numerous spirits in the ruins of what had been an old saloon. Molly O'Brien and Dancing Wind, just to be safe, put a white light of protection around themselves by visualizing a white light from GOD surrounding and protecting both of them. Then both women took their broad brimmed Western Stetsons off their heads and used the hats to knock the dust off themselves. Both women walked up to the saloon door as though the building was still standing and stepped inside.

★★Beginning in the 1880's to present time★★

Not much can surprise a gambler, and not much had surprised Jim Miller in the last century and a half. Jim Miller was a man who knew men, he knew when men were flush with money, and he knew when he had cleaned a man out of his last dollar. He always knew when another man was bluffing at poker or had a good hand and he should fold, and he was right most of the time. As a gambler he knew that an honest card game required the dealer to deal from the top of the deck of cards. A dishonest man might deal seconds, dealing the second card in the deck, or they might deal from the bottom of the deck. So when talking to a gambler, if one was to say: "Would you like me to deal from the top of the deck? " they would know you are a gambler too, and you will tell the truth or give them an honest game.

Jim sat around the poker table dealing five card stud to the other men and women sitting with him. Jim knew how the game would play out. Jim could tell who had a good poker hand. He knew who would fold. Nothing much surprised Jim as he was very good at reading people, as he leaned back in his chair giving his cards a quick glance, he turned his attention to reading the faces of the other poker players. Juan was a rich man's son, Pablo was a sheep herder. Maria was a nice woman who was trained to please men after she was sold to the saloon owner by her dad for five dollars and a bottle of whiskey. Sanchez was the man who owned the Water Hole Saloon. Carlos was the previous owner who had built the saloon at a waterhole along the Santa Fe Trail where travelers stopped to water their livestock and quench their own thirst with a drink of beer or whiskey. He had chosen a good business location.

Carlos made a fatal mistake when he let Sanchez buy him a glass of corn whiskey. As Carlos tipped back his head to swallow the glass of whiskey, Sanchez had positioned himself behind Carlos so as to catch Carlos by surprise as Sanchez silently and repeatedly knifed Carlos in the back. This was Sanchez's manner of killing innocent men who stopped at the saloon for a drink. People in the area knew that travelers with money and livestock were unlikely to leave Sanchez's saloon alive! Many frontier men and women who traveled without the protection of large groups of companions or wagon trains never left the Watering Hole Saloon alive. Their wagons or horses might be for sale to the next wagon train of travelers along the Santa Fe Trail. The dead men's money found its way into Sanchez's pockets.

Jim Miller had come to the Watering Hole Saloon to fleece the travelers along the Santa Fe Trail of their hard earned money. In return for Jim giving Sanchez twenty five percent of his profits, Sanchez allowed the gambler to work a table in his saloon. This arrangement suited both men until Jim talked of leaving. When Sanchez knew that Jim planned on leaving, he decided to kill him so as to have all of the money Jim had made. Sanchez had two thugs grab each of Jim Miller's arms and hold him for the minute it took him to knife the unsuspecting gambler in the back. As Jim Miller's lifeless body lay dying on the saloon floor, his confused spirit left his body and went over to the poker table where he was used to playing his card games. In time, Jim Miller's confused spirit returned to what was most familiar and what he often enjoyed doing, playing cards.

Juan was a spoiled rich man's son who had run off with the prettiest senorita in the village. A good liar, Juan made Juanita many promises, including marriage, but after she had given him his sexual satisfaction, Juan told Juanita that a man of his position could never consider marrying a servant girl. Juanita was a young teenager in love with Juan, but he broke her heart when he told her they would never marry. She knew that she should have left Juan right there but she was ashamed of what her family would say if she returned home and was no longer a virgin. Instead of the marriage she was promised, it was clear to her that Juan was just an immature young man who thought only of himself.

When Juan and Juanita stopped at the Watering Hole Saloon, Sanchez was outside on the front porch to welcome travelers inside. Juanita had a feeling that something was wrong, she begged Juan to leave now, but Juan would not hear of it. Instead he went inside and ordered a drink. When Sanchez, who was serving liquor from behind the bar saw Juan's coin purse full of gold he went around beside Juan and offered him a free drink of whiskey. As Juan went to drink his glass of whiskey, two of Sanchez's thugs quickly grabbed his arms, and Sanchez knifed him in the back. Terrified, Juanita ran screaming from the bar. She ran to the west trying to reach the shelter of the piñon forest where she could hide. Juanita only made it about fifty feet past the stable when the two thugs from the bar caught up with her. A pair of assassins murdered the woman with their knives. Juanita's spirit was caught up in the horror of witnessing the murder of Juan, and then being attacked and killed herself. In her spirit's confusion and terror, it would replay the last minutes of her life again and again.

After checking to see that his thugs had murdered Juanita by the stable, Sanchez returned to the bar. In front of the bar, lay Juan on the floor dying from his numerous knife wounds. Sanchez thought he better not have dying men lying around on the floor; he still might have more customers at his saloon today! Sanchez lifted the trap door in the floor of the saloon and threw Juan into the cellar where he died.

Pablo was a sheep herder who owned fifty sheep. Pablo thought he was getting a good deal when he decided to trade one of his sheep for a hot meal, a bottle of whiskey, and a night in bed with one of the saloon woman. He got his hot meal, his bottle of whiskey, and most of the night in bed with one of the saloon women. Instead of Pablo giving Sanchez one sheep as they had both agreed; Sanchez took all of Pablo's sheep and Pablo's life too!

When Maria was eleven years old, her dad took her to town. Maria's dad had wanted a son and all his wife could do was give him was a girl. Who would want a girl! What good is a girl! They cannot protect the sheep from hungry wolves. They can't plow the fields! They can't chop wood all day long! He needed a drink! Why had GOD cursed him with a girl? He left the Watering Hole Saloon with a bottle of whiskey, and the five dollars he had sold his daughter for. With Maria gone there was one less mouth to feed. When he got home he would just tell his wife that Maria had run away.

Everyone knew that Sanchez was in a good mood that day. Why else would Sanchez let a man who raised sheep and owned a farm walk out of his bar alive with five dollars in his pocket! That was not like Sanchez to let any money leave his bar! Yes, buying the Spanish girl Maria for five dollars had put Sanchez in a good frame of mind. He was thinking of all the money he would make charging his customers for spending the night with Maria.

Sanchez was an easy man to understand. If you had money or anything of value, Sanchez would try and steal it, or kill you for it whenever he could safely do so. The thugs and outlaws working for Sanchez lived only as long as Sanchez valued their work more than he valued their money. If one of his partners in crime had too much gold or silver, then Sanchez simply killed them too, and recruited new thugs. Throughout Sanchez's life he had a selfish and uncontrollable greedy attitude. Sanchez completely lacked integrity, dignity, honor, trust and respect for all life. Sanchez and men working for Sanchez slaughtered dozens of men and women. Most of the people murdered in and around the Watering Hole Saloon were able to find their way, with their Guardian Angel's help, to return *home* after they were murdered. In the end, the thugs lost the money they robbed and murdered to get; as it was robbed and stolen from them. When the dust settled, you could say that the thugs got what they had coming.

There are individuals today whose goal in life is to murder as many people as they can. When acts of evil are done, their Guardian Angels will literally back out of a room, going right through the walls to get away from these misguided spirits. Their Angels will not help them, and they do not want to be associated with such wrongful acts!

Then there are also people today whose goal in life is to help or teach as many people as they can. Their Angels will do all they can to guide them and help them achieve their goals. Their actions bring a smile to a Guardian Angel's face! Some of these individuals, the lucky the ones, who apply GOD's loving lessons, may have the gift of speaking to Angels!

In your life the choice is yours! To do right with others, to help someone whose car is broken down on the road, to feed the needy, to offer a helping hand, to set positive and creative actions into motion are all choices you have in this life! Often individuals have numerous chances to help or ignore people every week. The actions you take to help people you see in need reflect your compassion for your fellow man or woman.

★★Present time period★★

Molly O' Brian and Dancing Wind walked through the door and into the saloon. Both women stopped about three feet inside the door and looked around. The gambler at the table watched out of the corner of his eye as the two young women walked into the saloon. But with over one hundred and fifty years of experience, he knew that these kinds of people that occasionally drove through this town, seldom stopped. And if they did stop for a few minutes, they would not talk to him. These people were rude, because they ignored you and acted like they did not see you talking to them. These occasional strangers were really stupid because they could not see the saloon, the stable or the thirty nine spirits of the men and women living there!

Clearly these visitors were different. As Molly O' Brian and Dancing Wind walked across the saloon floor; Molly smiled at the gambler Jim

Miller. Then she winked at him as he watched her walk by him. Jim was so surprised that you could have knocked him over with a feather, and in fact, the chair he had been leaning back in suddenly crashed over backwards to the floor. She saw him! She actually saw him! Jim stood up and dropped his hand of cards on the table and walked over to Molly O' Brian.

When Dancing Wind saw the effect Molly was having on the gambler and the other spirits in the saloon she decided to back up her partner's play. Dancing Wind looked around at the saloon full of spirits. There were thirty four spirits scattered throughout the area, four were outside by the stable, and one spirit was behind the bar, Sanchez! Sanchez was in no hurry to offer the women a drink. In fact, Sanchez would have tried to attack them except for that white light of protection he saw around them. All the other spirits kept their distance from Sanchez. There was definitely no lost love between the thirty eight other spirits here and the one spirit called Sanchez! Since Dancing Wind considered Sanchez the most dangerous and the most likely to cause them problems, Dancing Wind kept her eye on Sanchez while positioning herself to protect Molly!

When Jim Miller, the gambler, walked up to Molly everyone in the bar stopped their conversations to watch the exchange! Jim stopped in front of Molly and straight out asked Molly, *"Why does everyone ignore me, or pretend I am not here?"* Molly paused for a moment to listen to her Guardian Angel standing beside her. After listening to what the Angel told her, Molly replied: "Would you like me to deal the hand of cards to you right off the top of the deck? " Jim replied, *"Yes, I would like that."* Then Molly replied, "You are dead, and now in a spirit's form. That is why most living people, do not see you," Jim replied, *"Oh, I did not know! "*

Then Molly explained to Jim it was time he went *home,* and she would like to help him. Even though Molly and Jim were talking, Molly knew that everyone else in the Watering Hole Saloon was listening to what was being said. Jim asked Molly: *"When can I go home?"* "Why not today!" Molly replied. Jim told her he could not pay Molly as Sanchez had taken all his money. Molly replied, "I will help all of you that choose to go *home,* you do not need to pay me anything!"

Why don't you and your friends come and meet me over at the old camp about five hundred feet to the west of town about thirty minutes before sunset, and I will help all of you go *home* who wish to! The reason why Molly was moving the spirits away from the saloon was to reduce the negative influence that Sanchez would cause. She knew that Sanchez would not want to have anything to do with the Angels or going anywhere near them! Molly thought it likely that Sanchez would stay in the saloon. And so it was that Sanchez chose to avoid the Angels. To this day Sanchez is still at the saloon! Before leaving, Molly went from spirit to spirit giving them encouragement and calming their fears. Following her Guardian Angel's advice and counsel, she gave them each the individual attention they required.

Molly spoke to Carlos, and she encouraged him to move on and start over, "Let Sanchez have the saloon, it is in ruins now," she said. The adobe saloon had returned to the dust or dirt of the earth. "Why hold on to hating Sanchez if it only makes you miserable?" "The love of GOD and his Angels is so much nicer. I promise you, GOD's unconditional love is waiting for you tonight, just inside and on the other side of the Tunnel of Light. Just let go of your hate for the people who have hurt you. Give love a chance to enter your life. When you have a choice to display anger and hate, is it really that nice? Do you really enjoy hating anyone? Are the best times in your life filled with anger and hate or when you are experiencing the real enjoyment of a friend, a companion, or lover?" Molly calmed Carlos's fear and anger as though they were lifelong friends talking with each other. And they would be lifelong friends because when the time came for Molly to return home, Carlos knew that he too would be there at the Door of Light with the Angels to welcome *home* the woman who had taken the time and had showed him the love to help him go *home*!

Molly spoke to Pablo and told him: "Take a look around. Your sheep are long gone. There is not any reason to remain here. The people you loved have gone *home*. It is time to go back to the people who love you." She told him his old friends would be waiting for him, and if he required any help two Angels would be there to help him go *home*. She told Pablo that if he still wanted to work as a sheep herder that she was sure that GOD would help find him some lost sheep he could watch over.

Molly then walked over to Maria and hugged her. As the tears ran down both of their cheeks, Molly could feel the pain and anger Maria held onto. The anger and resentment of being abandoned by her father and the way she was treated by every man in her life was keeping her on earth. Molly told Maria she had to let go of the anger at her dad for abandoning her! She had to let go of her hate for Sanchez and the way he treated her. She needed to let GOD's love inside her, and when she passed through the Door of Light, let the Angels' love just fill her to overflowing. She told Maria that her mother knew she did not run away, and she was waiting for her now to show Maria all the love she has for her daughter! When Maria looked into the Tunnel of Light she would see her mother and her Guardian Angel there to accompany her *home*! Maria whispered into Molly's ear one Spanish word, *"Gracias"* *(Thank you)*. Then they both cried in each other's arms as they hugged each other and let GOD's love flow all about them.

Molly went up to Juan and told him the money that Sanchez had murdered him for was gone! It was not here for him to get back! That money had been in turn stolen from Sanchez. Sanchez had been killed by a man he was trying to rob. Why stay here? It is time to get on with your life. Review the lessons you have learned with your Angels and start over! GOD gives everyone a second chance! Why don't you make the most of it?

Juan then realized that there was no reason for him to stay on earth any more. Juan decided to go *home*. In the evening, he would go see if the story of the Angels was true.

Then Molly when out to the stable where four more spirits were reliving the trauma and fear of their murders. Molly began talking with Juanita who had been knifed as she fled running for the safety of the forest to the west. Molly calmed the woman down, calming her fear and holding her trembling body. Molly helped her to see her Guardian Angel who had been there for her all the time. Juanita was angry at Juan getting her into this mess, as well as lying that he would marry her if she would slip off together with him. Together Molly and Juanita talked about how it was time to let go of her fear as well as her anger at Juan for getting her into this mess in the first place. She did not need to hold on to this world or this life any more. Why not begin again with a fresh start. It was time she left here, and they would help her today as they walked with her to the west away from the stables. The three other spirits in the stable heard the comforting words and they too accompanied them.

As the sun set in the western sky, Dancing Wind invited all the spirits to come over and watch the sunset with her. Dancing Wind built a small fire. She began playing the flute softly and slowly as she walked around in a large circle with the small fire in the center of her circle. The spirits were drawn to the beautiful melody that filled them with love and joy.

Behind Dancing Wind, more and more spirits came to join in with her, and began following her as she circled the fire playing her flute. Molly O' Brian sat on the ground and began drumming on the handmade Indian drum, which had been a gift to her from her spiritual teacher. Slowly Molly picked up the pace faster and faster. Then beside the circle, a Door of Light suddenly appeared and opened with an Angel standing guard on each side. One by one, the spirits approached the two Angels and cautiously peered into the doorway. It was true! Their loved ones were waiting for them! One at a time they looked into and then entered the Tunnel of Light where they were joined by their loved ones waiting for them! When the spirits had all gone *home* to GOD; the two Angels standing guard on each side of the Door of Light entered inside. Suddenly the Door of Light disappeared. Dancing Wind stopped playing her flute and Molly quit drumming.

The two women smiled and hugged each other. Molly poured water from her canteen on the fire putting it out completely. Then walking silently back to their vehicle, they started up the jeep as the sun set in the reddish western sky. Both women reinforced their white light of protection around themselves and their jeep as they drove off silently lost in their thoughts about the day's events. But there was one thing Molly knew, as she raced her Jeep Wrangler on the dirt roads towards Santa Fe; there was a rare steak waiting for her at the T-bone Steak House, and she and Dancing Wind had earned it.

Love is like a rainbow
All across the sky
Love is like a rainbow
A beauty to the eye
Love is like a rainbow
When you give a helping hand
Love is like a rainbow

A Lesson in Prospecting for Gold

An old prospector friend of mine

Around the campfire there were four prospectors telling stories about the gold they found, dreamed of finding, as well as the lost gold deposits that were still out there to be found. Then that old prospector had to tell that impossible story. He knew the prospector was a dam liar! The trouble was he was shaking as the prospector told the story and even a month later he could think of nothing else in his free time except the story the old prospector told him about watching this Indian girl tracking an ancient trail. He said he saw this teenage girl tracking in the mountains to the west of the Stollsteimer River in southern Colorado. He had watched her for two hours and had come to believe she was tracking an old trail which she occasionally lost, and then she acquired the trail again and continued on. Finally he had gone over to ask the teenager what she was doing.

She told him she was tracking the trail of some outlaws as they came down out of the mountains to the west. She was tracking them to their campsite where they spent the night. While he saw horses and horse tracks along the Piedra River and the Stollsteimer River, she was not following any horse tracks he could see. When he asked her, "Well about how long ago did the riders come through here," she told him, "About a hundred and fifty years ago! "He said, "You're joking, right? " She told him, "No, I am quite serious. The trail I am following was made in approximately 1856! "She told him she was tracking the trail of four outlaws who were killed by Ute Indians just to the west of the Stollsteimer River and the Piedra River about a mile north of the junction where the two rivers came together.

The old man had thought of nothing else for the last two months. How can anyone track a trail that was made over a century ago? He knew it was impossible! It just simply was not possible! But he simply could not let go of the thought. He could not get the implications of that story out of his mind. He knew that there probably was no such

Indian girl anyway. Only an old fool or a prospector could believe such a crazy story! The story this man heard was impossible; that this girl had tracked the trail of some outlaws that were wiped out by Ute Indians up on the Stollsteimer River, east of Durango, Colorado in the 1800's! Any idiot knew it is very hard to follow a horses trail through the San Juan Mountains if you were an hour behind the horseman. Possibly a very skilled Apache tracker could follow a trail a week old. Now everyone knows it is impossible to follow some outlaws through the San Juan Mountains when they have a hundred and fifty year head start!

After two months the old man decided he would check out the story about the Arapaho tracker. Mind you, he knew that there was nothing to the story, and he was perfectly sure that he was not going to waste his gas on this fool's story. He made $342 a month on his social security and he was not going to spend $125 of it driving his old pickup up to Abiquiu looking for some teenager who did not exist anyway! In addition he could not risk getting stopped in a road block where they might ask him for proof of insurance on his truck. Those state police were crazy. They expected you to have insurance on your vehicle!

How is someone living on $342 supposed to have auto insurance? His heart medicine was $107 a month, and that was just to keep him alive! That left him $235 a month to live on! That's $57 a week to pay his housing, meals, gas and doctors bills! He was good at fixing rice and beans and tortillas to live on. Occasionally he got a rabbit or a rattle snake with his .22 rifle, so he had some meat to throw on the tortillas or in a pot of beans. Sometimes he could get some vegetables from the dumpsters behind the supermarkets. But the prospector did not like going through the dumpsters very much as he smelled bad after going through the rotten produce trying to find some useable vegetables.

It was hard being old; no one wanted to hire you. He did not have much money to live on. Times had been really hard lately! What the old man needed, what any prospector needs; is a placer gold deposit that he could work to make a little money on the side! It could be a dry placer he could work with a dry washer to recover the gold. It could be a placer deposit in a stream that he shoveled the gravel into a sluice box. He wanted some place remote where he would be left alone to work in peace and where the E. P. A. (Environmental Protection Agency) or the B. L. M. (Bureau of Land Management) would not find him. What he needed was a change of luck. He needed a miracle if he wanted to be able to start eating twice a day! He so desperately wanted to replace his bare thread clothes, to be able to afford a dinner out in a nice restaurant. It just was not easy to be old and slow when no one wanted to hire you to work.

So in desperation the old prospector hitchhiked up north to find the teenage girl called Dancing Wind. He came prepared for the journey north with his backpack, a bedroll, toilet paper, a compass, matches, an old tattered road map, and nine burritos he had made with beans, rice and tortillas he had put in an old paper bag and he carried a canteen of water. He also brought along his coffee pot and some chicory roots he had dried to make coffee. He simply could not afford any coffee this month. Just for luck he brought along his gold pan too. He could always use it to wash up, should he find a stream or river to camp by. Of course, he would pan any streams he saw for gold.

From his camp on some vacant land outside La Mesilla he planned to hitchhike north on Interstate 25. In two days he reached Albuquerque. The next day his luck held and he got a ride to Santa Fe in the morning and another ride to Espanola in the afternoon.

He spent the night camped in the woods along the Rio Grande and the next morning he arrive in Abiquiu. In three and a half days, he had eaten seven burritos. He skipped lunch to make his food last longer. He felt pretty good as he filled his canteen at the general store in Abiquiu. He drank lots of water to fill up his empty stomach. He had a full canteen of water and he still had two of his burritos. With luck he might find that Arapaho Indian today.

At the general store in town, which is the only store in town, he asked a number of people where to find the Indian girl who tracks trails. Someone suggested asking at the library. There the librarian directed him to her old brown trailer above the plaza. The old prospector thought that if you took away the cars and the electric lines, Abiquiu looked like any Mexican town might have a century ago. As he walked across the dirt plaza there were four cows looking for grass to eat. On the north side of the plaza was on old brown adobe (dried mud and straw bricks) Spanish style church. In the plaza in front of the church was a white wooden cross.

At the trailer he knocked on the door and then he heard the barking of a dog. The door opened and there stood a skinny Arapaho Indian teenager. The girl had long black hair going down to her waist and she was holding back a large reddish brown Chesapeake Bay Retriever which growled like it wanted a piece of his hide. She asked him, "What do you want? " The prospector asked if he could come inside. She told him no, but she would come outside and talk with him if he liked. Dancing Wind held the protective dog's collar in one hand to maintain control while she sat down with the old prospector to talk with him.

Dancing Wind sat down on her wooden porch with the old prospector. She was learning to track. She was a tracker at heart, so she started to track with the old-timer who had come to her door. She noticed the old clothes he wore, his worn out boots, the old canvas backpack which just about looked empty. She saw the signs of hunger, and she felt the old man's desperation. He was literally at the end of his rope; he had no one else to turn to for help. Dancing Wind didn't know what to do so she started talking to the old-timer asking what he enjoyed doing, what kind of work he was doing and why he had come to see her.

Mark was the old prospector's name. He had been named after the Mark in the Bible his parents used to read before they had passed away. In his younger days Mark had done odd jobs, whatever it took to put food on the table. He had done logging, tree planting,worked as a migrant worker harvesting crops from farmers' fields. He had wrangled horses, done carpentry work, house framing, sheet rocking, and painting, and most importantly he enjoyed prospecting for gold.

He no longer had the strength or speed to keep up with the younger workers in the construction industry. The hard labor jobs like working at logging, tree planting, and breaking wild horses were just too difficult for him now. He could not take more broken bones from being thrown from a wild horse! His youth, vibrant energy, and strength were simply part of his past as he had grown into the winter of his years.

The old prospector talked about his prospecting for gold in Aravaca, Arizona. Here he had dry washed for gold. He shoveled the dirt into the dry washer where he used his hand to operate air bellows to blow out the dry dirt. He picked out the rocks by hand. The gold, when there was any gold to be found was trapped in the raffles or slats of the dry washer. With hard work, a man could make $20 a day. But the best locations had been claimed in mining claims so they were no longer available for him to work.

In the 1970's he had worked on the Yukon River up in Alaska. Mark told how there was good gold to be found up on the Yukon River. In places, one could pan 20-60 small flakes of gold dust in each pan with his gold pan. Yes that was good gold! Once down on Cherry Creek he had hit a nice streak of pay dirt. He had located a twenty foot stretch of virgin gravel on bedrock that had never been touched. In three hours with his 2 ½ inch gold dredge powered by a three horsepower lawn mower engine he had recovered two five gallon plastic buckets of gold and black sands. Of course, he had a partner who had never been placer gold mining before who in return for him teaching him how to mine gold had provided the food or grubstake for the trip. As partners they split everything they found 50-50. They both got an equal share of the gold.

With the two buckets of gold and black sands Mark went to find a spot on Cherry Creek to sit down beside the water and pan his gold. His partner had told Mark: "I can pan gold so I will take the second bucket and pan it."

Mark asked, "Are you sure you can do this? "

His partner told Mark, "No problem. I know how to pan gold."

So they each took one bucket of the gold and black sands and sitting on the banks of the flowing water about two hundred feet apart, they panned the contents of their buckets. A half hour later Mark finished his very careful panning of his bucket and he had ten ounces of gold. At $200 an ounce they would get in the town of Eagle when they sold their gold, they should have $2,000 each!

When Mark finished up panning his bucket, he went over to watch his partner finish up the last of his bucket of gold. As he walked up, he saw his partner grab up a hand full of gold nuggets and send them flying out into the stream. He threw them away! Mark was so shocked, that his mouth just fell wide open and he could only point at his partner's gold pan as he took the last handful of the gold nuggets and sent them flying into the stream. Outrage filled him. Mark wanted to shoot his partner! They had worked for weeks, panning on numerous gravel bars along the Yukon River to locate this good site. His partner had just thrown away $1,900 in gold nuggets then proudly turned to him and pointed out the half ounce ($100) of gold dust he had saved! When he had been taught to pan gold he had only been shown how to catch the fine gold dust. He simply did not recognize the gold nuggets so he had thrown away all the gold nuggets in his bucket!

Mark told how when he had told his partner he had ten ounces of gold he had gotten from his bucket.

When he asked his partner how much gold he had, his partner patted Mark on the back and said let's see, "You have ten ounces of gold, and I have a half ounce so the total amount of gold is 10. 5 ounces of gold divided by two is 5 ¼ ounces of gold for each of us. You see old timer, we are partners so we share everything equally! "

When Dancing Wind asked why he was no longer mining placer gold up on the Yukon River of Alaska he told her. It was now part of the Yukon/Charlie Park and they did not allow him to use his gold dredge in the park. The last trip up river he had been approached at his camp on the river by a boat load of Yukon Charlie Park Rangers, these officials asked him what he was doing. Since his gold dredge was in plain sight he simply told them the truth. He was gold mining. The park ranger's employees told him that it was illegal to mine gold in their park, and if they ever caught him again in the park mining gold they would kill him!

Yes, it was time to move on. Where hundreds of independent men used to be mining gold along the Yukon River and its tributaries, working their small gold dredges making a living, there now are none. The Park Rangers moved them out! Only the large mining companies seem to have the ability and financial resources to deal with the B. L. M. and get the needed permits. The natural resources of gold are so abundant there along the Yukon, there could easily be full-time employment for several thousand men and women. Instead of helping the small miners and working with them, it seems that the B. L. M. and the US Park Service just drives the small gold miners out of business.

Mark told me that the last patent on a placer mining claim that he was aware of was issued to a small placer gold miner by the B. L. M. in Alaska to the gold miner twenty years after he died! It was issued to the next of kin.

When Dancing Wind asked about any location the old prospector liked a lot, he told her about a prospecting trip he had made into the Tecolote Mountains (Owl Mountains) of old México. Dancing Wind asked the prospector if he would join her for lunch. When he agreed to join her for lunch, she went inside the trailer and made some soup and five ham and cheese sandwiches. She would later tell him her appetite was just not what she expected. Even when making the sandwiches, she intended to let Mark take two extra sandwiches with him when he left. She was just trying to be polite about giving him the two extra sandwiches. The old prospector enjoyed the soup and eating two of the sandwiches, it was the best meal he had had in days. After eating the soup and two sandwiches Mark continued with his story.

Mark and another prospector Jerry Campbell had prospected down in the Tecolote (Owl) Mountains back in the 1980's—about twenty five years ago. They were looking for placer gold. The mountains were very hot and dry and located in the Sonoran Desert. They had seen evidence of old Spanish mining but nothing recent. While they could find gold in the washes, it was not enough to make a living dry washing for placer gold dust. Mark always felt in his gut that there were some good gold pockets in the Owl Mountains.

Then Mark told Dancing Wind about the bet he had with his partner Jerry Campbell. They had each bet each other that each one of them would discover a rich placer gold deposit first. The loser of the bet had to buy the winner of the bet every meal for the next thirty days at any restaurant the winner chose anywhere in the United States! Unfortunately, neither man was able to win the bet, as they did not find a rich placer gold deposit. For years they had joked with each other about the bet.

Now Dancing wind could begin to understand the problem the two prospectors had!

The joke, the bet, told it all to her—it was the thinking and the attitude of the two prospectors which doomed there effort to failure. They were just going into the mountains to plunder the mountain's gold! They did not plan to make any effort to help the environment. They had no plans to help the animals, the plants, or Mother Earth with any of the gold that they might recover. They made NO effort to work with the nature spirits, to help the mountains, to help the plants or animals. To change their results the old prospector would have to change his approach and attitude if he was to achieve the results he desired.

So Dancing Wind leaned back on the 4x4 porch post and thought a few minutes about the problem she faced were she to help the old prospector. If, as she spoke with the old-timer; if she felt real change was possible, she would try and help him. Should he be unwilling to change his thinking, his attitude, and to follow her advice, she would drop him like a hot potato right out of a 350 degree oven!

And so she began talking with Mark directly, bluntly and forcefully. She told him:

"The reason you are such a poor prospector, Mark, is your attitude! You go into a mountain range like it is yours; like you own it. You literally act like it is yours, to do or treat like you wish. *NOTHING IN THOSE MOUNTAINS IS YOURS! ABSOLUTELY NOTHING!* You can say it belongs to The Creator, or you might say to Mother Earth, or possibly the nature spirits, the trees, plants or animals that live in those mountains and take care of them! It certainly is not yours! Even if you buy the land, it is NOT yours! If not for The Creator or

Mother Earth, there would not be plants or animals living in those mountains."

Then the teenage girl told him a story as an Angel whispered it into her ear. "A couple of centuries ago the Spanish came into the Tecolote (Owl) Mountains to plunder the gold. They came with a lust for gold, and slaughtered the environment-- destroying the plants, the animals, digging pits, and raping the landscape! "Dancing Wind told the old prospector, *"MAKE NO MISTAKE ABOUT IT, THERE WILL ALWAYS BE CONSEQUENCES TO YOUR ACTIONS!" THERE ARE ALWAYS CONSEQUENCES; EITHER CREATIVE OR DESTRUCTIVE, TO ONES ACTIONS! GOOD OR POSITIVE ACTIONS WILL RESULT IN NICE CONSEQUENCES. "NEGATIVE OR BAD ACTIONS WILL ALWAYS REAP NEGATIVE CONSEQUENCES YOU CERTAINLY DO NOT WANT TO EXPERIENCE!'*

"When the Spanish came into the Tecolote Mountains they raped the land digging holes, and destroying the vegetation which controlled the erosion. They cut down the trees. The deer, javelinas (wild pigs), and even the owls found their way into the Spanish cooking pots. The owls which kept the mice population down low were easy to kill as they had never even seen or learned of the danger of being shot by a rifle. With a reckless disregard for Mother Earth, they took whatever they wanted without asking Mother Nature's permission. '

"With the ecosystem knocked out of balance; the mouse population exploded. The mice were carriers of bubonic plague! The mice entered the Spaniards' camp, getting into their bedding and cleaning up the plates of food while the Spaniards worked the mountains to get all the gold they could. Wherever the mice went in the Spanish miners' camp, they spread the bubonic plague! '

"Soon the Spaniards came down with bubonic plague! It started with a fever which would not go away. Then came pain in the abdominal area, along with pain under their arms and in their testacies. Soon they began pissing blood. Then they had blood in their stools when they went to the bathroom. Next their tongues turned black, they ran a high fever and died. All the Spaniards died! The Spanish miners literally reaped what they sowed! I am not telling you this to scare you. I am telling you this to impress upon you the need to help the earth and the plants and animals. There are always consequences to your actions. You will reap what you sow! If you want the help of the Nature Spirits and the Angels you better be willing to work with them and meet them half way! '

"In your case, let me ask you, when you go into a mountain range to prospect what specific actions do you take to help the animals, the plants and to improve the environment? Do you feed the birds? Have you put out a salt block near by the water holes? Have you cleaned out the water holes or springs? Have you planted dry land grass to control erosion and give the animals more food? Have you planted trees in the mountains? Have you planted asparagus plants or seed? Have you planted fruit trees to help the plants, the animals, and any lost people who should come by? In the cold mountain lakes have you planted wild rice to help the ducks, geese, and lost humans who need food to eat? The prospector looked down at his feet; he could not look the teenage girl in the eyes as he could not tell her he had helped the mountains, the plants or the animals. 'His behavior had been lacking in helping the environment, and she knew it; that is why the Angel talking to the girl had told her to ask these questions.

Then Dancing Wind told the old prospector that it was time he changed if he wanted to change his luck in prospecting. He needed to think about what he could do to help the Tecolote Mountains if he wanted the help of the Nature Spirits and the Angels.

So Dancing Wind told him to think about what he was willing to do to help Mother Earth. "I want to hear a carefully thought out plan you will carry out to help the mountains. Included in this plan should be the salt blocks you plan to place up by the springs, the tinajas you plan to build to catch water when it rains so the animals have new water sources, the trees you plan to plant to help the environment— and those trees need to be appropriate to the available water supply. If you are in a dry area, you need to plant plants that can tolerate low rainfall amounts. '

"Are there dry land native grasses you can plant like Gama and Buffalo grass? Can you plant fruit trees and fence them to protect the trees and have the overflow from a spring or tinaja (a natural rock formation which holds water) water the trees? Is there sufficient rainfall in your area? Can you plant cottonwood trees, oak trees, or raspberry plants? In northern mountain lakes can you plant wild rice. You need to plant the fresh seed from a nursery as the dry wild rice you see in stores will not germinate and grow. If you are going to pick up the trash, where are you going to take it so it does not litter up a new area? I want you to seriously consider a plan you are going to carry out, and then we will talk about a trip into the Tecolote Mountains of Mexico. '

★★★★

In the fall of the year, Dancing Wind traveled with the old prospector into the Tecolote Mountains of Mexico. On the south end of the mountain range near the crest of the mountains is a small spring. Together they cleaned out the spring. They removed the trash men had thrown in the water as well as old leaves and cleaned out the mud so that the water could flow from the spring down the hill and water the trees and grass below the spring.

They asked the spring to provide its life giving water to the three trees seedlings they had carried into the mountains, as well as the grass they were spreading below the spring. They also asked the spring to provide its life giving water to the plants, animals, and humans in need. They had also carried up a salt block for use by the animals watering at the spring. This salt was placed near the spring but out of sight of a casual human visitor.

Then they prayed to GOD, the nature spirits, the Angels and also to Mother Earth for their blessing on the plants that they had planted and that the spring would provide an abundance of safe drinking water. They also asked for permission to prospect in the mountains for placer gold. When they received permission from the Nature Spirits to prospect for placer gold, they asked where they should go. The Angels then directed them to look east, up to the ridge line above them. They then pointed out the boundaries of where the prospector should use his dry washer. They also bounded their directions; telling him to stay east of the wash or arroyo to the west. The Angels had suggested about one square mile of the rugged Tecolote Mountains as where the prospector should work. In practice, the area of the mountain slopes all drained into one wash. Both of them gave a prayer of thanks.

The old prospector now knew where he should work to use his dry washer to recover placer gold. He was very happy for the counsel of the Angels. He then drove Dancing Wind back to La Mesilla where she had left her jeep. Dancing Wind was happy she had been able to get the old prospector to consider helping Mother Earth and try to help the environment. She was happy he had a good place to work to make a little money he desperately needed.

As Dancing Wind drove north on I-25 towards Abiquiu, she wondered about one thing. The Angels had told her there were seven sites in the Tecolote Mountains where the Spanish mined gold centuries ago. The Angels had also said that there were nine sites in the Tecolote Mountains with gold. So that implied that there were two rich untouched virgin gold deposits. Did GOD's Angels put the old prospector on one of the Spanish sites or onto one of the rich virgin gold deposits? Dancing Wind would not ask the Angels because she knew they had put the old prospector on the deposit that was right or appropriate for him.

As Dancing Wind drove north, she looked to the right of her and there on the passenger seat was her Guardian Angel Lily smiling at her with her crooked smile. The Angel smiled at her and told Dancing Wind: *"You're coming along just fine"*. Then the Angel winked at her. Dancing Wind looked at the Angel sitting on the car seat beside her and smiled at the beautiful Angel. Then Dancing Winds eyes returned to the highway she was driving down. When she glanced at the seat beside her the Angel was gone. The only trace of the Angels presence was the wonderful feeling she felt. Dancing Wind smiled. Yes; it was a nice life lesson for her. She was just happy she could help the old man. Often in one's life, we encounter people who need someone who will care enough to give them a hot meal, a job, or a helping hand. Will you take the time to help the individual in need when you encounter them?

Beauty is on the Mountains
Beauty is on the Snow
Beauty is an Angel
When she is all Aglow

Mountain of the Witches

S ierra de los Brujos is the name the old Spanish people call the Mountain of the Witches. Here on this mountain, change was slow to come, but change was coming even here. The night wind spoke of the changes and the night owls spoke of the changes and watched the events unfold. Even the Angels knew that change was coming.

The Mountain of the Witches was accessible by a single, rocky and potholed, dirt road as long as it had not rained recently. When it rained, the mud holes would make the road impassable for days until the dirt road had time to dry out. Four wheelers might explore the road during the day, but they knew to hurry off the mountain before dark. Mountain of the Witches was not a mountain that you camped on overnight; or if you did, one never camped on the mountain twice, as the witches were known to come out at night! Their appearance after dark had a way of encouraging a very hasty departure by campers planning to spend the night upon their mountain. Several times a year the witches had sent campers fleeing in a hasty departure off their mountain.

The ducks and wildlife liked the solitude, so many ducks made their nest on the lake up on the mountain top. Bear made the tall pine and oak forest on the mountain their home which suited the witches' just fine because it discouraged any cattle rancher from running his cattle on the mountain. The ranchers did not want to lose their cattle and calves to the hungry bears. The witches liked the solitude, because they had a secret that they had been concealing for over two hundred and fifty years. It was a secret the witches intended to keep!

★★★★

The Arapaho teenager was taller than most Indian women at 5' 7". She weighed 117 pounds dripping wet out of the shower, and she moved with grace, her long black hair flowing down her back to her belt. While only a nineteen year old teenager, she was different than many teenagers. Dancing Wind often carried on conversations with Angels. Throughout every country on this Mother Earth there are also other teenagers who will take the time and make the effort to communicate with their Guardian Angels. This story is about two such teenagers, Dancing Wind and her good friend Molly O'Brien. Molly, too, was nineteen, but she had bright red hair and an Irish temper which sometimes exploded on anyone foolish enough to really piss her off. Together the two teenagers were the best of friends. Together they decided to track the old trails going up the Mountain of the Witches.

As the spirits on the top of Sierra de los Brujos watched, the two teenagers worked their way up the mountain. The spirits knew was trouble when they saw it. They could easily read the thoughts and know the intentions of the two trackers. The witches realized the teenage trackers were headed straight towards them! Very slowly the spirits on top of the mountain felt their apprehensions grow as the two girls tracked the trails up from the base of the tree covered mountain. For two centuries, the witches' reputation had stood the test of time to keep people away. In the days to come, their very reputation would be put to the test. Soon it would come down to all thirty eight witches using ever resource they had to scare those two teenage trackers off their mountain!

Dancing Wind knew the mountain's name and she knew the mountain's reputation. As a safety precaution she had asked GOD to put a white light of protection around her. Molly O'Brien followed her friend's example. Then after visualizing the white light of protection around her, she had thanked The Creator for the help. Then Dancing Wind and Molly O'Brien began tracking the trail higher and higher up the mountain slopes. They were tracking an Old Spanish Trail from the 1730-1750's, up the mountain slopes towards the mountain's crest.

On the top of the mountain the thirty eight spirits watched the teenage girls' progress as they tracked the old trail. When occasionally the girls lost the old trail, the spirits smiled at each other. When the teenagers picked up the old trail again the seventeen French spirits looked accusingly over at the twenty-one Spanish spirits. They had almost forgotten in over two centuries; but there in the back of their memories, they recalled the Spanish miners using Indian slaves to set up the rock monuments between their mine up in the mountains to the north and their cache site on the Mountain of the Witches where they had hidden the gold and silver bars from their mine.

The Frenchmen's' spirits looked accusingly at the Spanish spirits and their looks said it all, *"It is your fault again."* Never in over two hundred years had the French or Spanish spirits observed anyone following their rock monuments! The witches apprehension grew, this situation was going bad fast! It was like that Arapaho girl was talking to the rocks the way she tracked the trail! The Frenchmen blamed all their troubles on the Spanish. If they had not made the last raid on the Indian village to get more slaves to work in the mines this would not have happened!

★★Two hundred years ago★★

The Frenchmen had come from New Orleans out west to the Rocky Mountains to trap. Beaver for their pelts to make into beaver hats. Up in the mountains, west of Trinidad, Colorado, they had struck gold! They all planned to return to France as rich men. They agreed they would mine the gold until they each had four bars of gold. One bar of gold would buy them the lands they desired back in France, a second bar of gold would give them a very nice home to live out their lives and the third and fourth bar of gold would enable them to live very comfortably the rest of their lives.

Their plan had come apart as the first bar of molten gold was poured into the crude mold that formed the gold bar. Gold fever struck them – greed for more and more money. They all wanted more and more gold as they watched the first bright gold bar lifted out of the mold, and they each greedily handled it! No longer were four bars of gold enough!

The Spanish had also succumbed to gold fever when the Frenchmen had appeared at Mora, New Mexico needing to buy food, gun powder, and iron digging bars to work their gold mine. An agreement was reached between the Spanish and the Frenchmen to work the rich gold mine together and share the gold.

The Spanish wanted to learn the location of the source of the gold in the mountains, so that they could obtain it for themselves! The only way to do this was agree to supply the food, gun powder, and iron needed to work the mines. They would then insist that the gold needed to be stored nearby so that they could seize it for themselves! After all, this was really Spanish territory, claimed by the King of Spain, so it was only fair that all the gold should belong to them! They would tell the stupid Frenchmen that by storing the gold near Mora that they could watch over it in winter so it was not stolen and that when they were ready to return to New Orleans, that the Spanish Trail was more easily accessible from Mora than the high mountains in Colorado which would be snowed in during the winter.

The Frenchman wanted the food, gunpowder, and iron to work the mines. By working with the Spanish, they could get the supplies they desperately needed to mine more gold!

They knew that the Spanish would feel secure if the gold was stored near Mora. Their settlement would be close by. But the Spanish were fools if they felt that the French trappers did not know several ways off the mountains where they agreed to store the gold. When they left by the back way out of Mora, they would load the horses and mules with their gold and take the Spaniards gold too! They might as well take advantage of the free Spanish labor! Besides this was really a part of France when Cavalier la Salle claimed the land for the King of France 1682, so they were mining the gold in territory claimed by the King of France. Clearly they were working in New France as New Orleans was settled in 1718 by Sieu de Bienville! It was only right that the Frenchmen kept all the gold when they loaded up the pack animals for their return trip to New Orleans along the Old Spanish Trail!

So it was an agreement sealed by greed for gold that got the Frenchmen and the Spanish working together mining the gold. Once there at the mine, the Spanish showed the French how to greatly increase the mine's output by enslaving the Indians living nearby. They would attack the smaller family groups of Indians, killing off the tough warriors and telling the remaining Indian slaves that if they tried to escape that they would kill off their remaining family. When they attacked a small village, the French trappers, who were very good shots, used their skills to murder the Indian warriors. Then the Spanish would use their skills with a whip, beating and torturing the Indian slaves to get the maximum work out of them.

When the Indians died working in the mines, they just raided more Indian villages to get additional slaves for their mine. Over the years, as more and more bars of gold were produced from the rich mine, the greed and lust for gold by Spanish and French miners grew and grew. At first four gold bars was enough to supply their needs to live well when they returned to France or Spain. As the pile of gold bars grew bigger and bigger, then they wanted more and more gold. They had gold fever!

In the end, it was their greed and one lost Indian boy which led to losing all the gold and silver that they had worked and murdered to obtain. The French trappers had been off hunting for elk and deer to feed the slaves at the mine, when the Spaniards had decided to raid another small Indian village for more slaves. The raid had gone well. They captured or killed everyone in the village at the time, but three Cheyenne warriors had been off hunting for a lost teenage boy, and so they were not captured by the Spanish slave traders.

The three Cheyenne warriors anger knew no bounds when they

returned to their village, saw the burned camp, and their dead family members. Their kidnapped family members were not in sight. The Indian warriors knew how to track a trail, so they followed the trail back to the mines where their loved ones were being worked and beaten as slaves. They watched and observed, and made their plans. They would obtain justice or die trying!

It should have been impossible for three warriors accompanied by one teenage boy to attack an armed camp of fifty-four Spaniards and Frenchmen. But when individuals have been pushed to the limit, when they will fight for what they believe in and will not accept defeat or failure, they can stand against impossible odds. These Cheyenne would not accept any option but to free their families, their wives, and their children from the slavers. They planned to kill the French and Spanish miners or drive them from their land!

The Cheyenne started by ambushing a small group of Frenchman as they left the camp to go hunting for meat. They successfully carried out the ambush, killing three Frenchmen and one Spaniard. The Frenchmen and the Spaniard's spirits looked at their own lifeless bodies lying on the ground, and took off back to camp to warn the men about the ambush and to make sure no one took their share of gold!

When the spirits of the dead Spanish and French returned to camp, no one would listen to their warning about the four Cheyenne Indians. In fact, everyone in camp acted like they could not see or hear them! The living Spaniards and Frenchmen talked like the hunters were still gone! It was like their companions could not see or hear them at all! The stupid fools would not listen to the spirits of the dead men. They did not put out the extra guards as the dead men's spirits told them to do! So the spirits of the dead stayed in camp and watched over their gold! They tried to warn the camp guard who was watching the horses and mules about the Cheyenne warriors, but when sleep overcame him late at night, the Cheyenne warriors slipped up behind him and showed him that a black obsidian stone knife worked just fine to slit his throat. And so another Spaniard went into spirit. Another man guarding the horses that night died, when two arrows silently slammed into his body. When the morning sun awakened the miners' camp, they found two lifeless bodies of their companions and a dozen horses missing!

The Spanish and French doubled the guards on the camp and the horse herd and they discussed stopping the mining for the season, but greed overcame their caution and they decided to continue getting all the gold they could! Unknown to the men at camp, the spirits of their six dead companions were still there in the camp with them hearing every word and thought, of the men they had lived and worked with. They saw that some felt their loss, but most were not the least upset about their death. Underneath the sorrowful faces that they put on for the people around them, they were counting the gold bars in their mind and figuring that there were now more gold bars for them! The spirits stayed around the campfire and kept a close eye on their share of the gold bars. The spirits did not have the ability to lift a single gold bar. They could not buy food, clothes, a house, or land. They simply failed to realize that all the gold that they had fought and murdered to get was now useless to them. They were trapped by the gold as if they were chained to it; like they chained up their slaves. They were trapped by imaginary chains of greed for the gold and these chains were as strong as the toughest iron chains!

The Cheyenne warriors were not interested in the horses they had stolen except as offerings to other Cheyenne warriors they were able to enlist to help in attacking the Spanish and French miners, and to drive them from their land and free their families! It took the Cheyenne warriors about two weeks to return to the mine site. When they returned, there were twelve warriors instead of the original four

Cheyenne. They were still outnumbered by the miners over four to one! The Cheyenne would also have to use all their fighting skills since they did not have that many rifles. The rifles that their enemies carried could reach out and kill them from two hundred yards away! The Cheyenne warriors had three major goals: kill their enemies that had kidnapped and murdered their families, free their remaining family members, and steal the horses. So they watched and learned the habits of their enemies as they watched the camp from the concealment of the surrounding forest and mountains.

The Spanish and French had started to grow sloppy in guarding the camp. They had been watchful at first, but after two weeks and not seeing any Indians about, they were getting lazy about guarding the camp. The Cheyenne planned a surprise attack at the crack of dawn to free their brothers held prisoner and also to steal more horses.

The Cheyenne warriors moved in as close to camp as possible to take advantage of their shorter range bows and arrows. They planned to try and free as many family members as possible and kill anyone trying to stop them. On the opposite side of the camp other Cheyenne warriors would be killing the guards, watching the horses, and making off with as many horses as possible.

Six warriors went for the horses. They came in and hit hard and fast just as the early morning first light appeared, when they could accurately fire their arrows into the enemy.

While the surprise was not complete, one guard was restless and had been awake, his two companions were not as fortunate when Cheyenne arrows slammed into them. Unfortunately the one guard who was awake also awakened the entire camp in alarm when he fired his rifle at one of the Cheyenne warriors killing him.

The rifle shot woke up the Spanish and French miners and they stood up and grabbed their rifles. While looking towards the horse herd, the second group of Cheyenne warriors unleashed a fury of arrows. They were unable to get into camp to free their families. They killed three men and wounded five more. Then the Cheyenne were forced to withdraw under heavy rifle fire.

The French and Spanish miners were scared. For the first time, they were really scared! It was as if the vibration or smell of fear rolled around the entire camp. If they wanted to get out with their gold they felt they had to go now! With six men killed two weeks earlier and five more men dying today, they wanted out and they wanted the safety of the Spanish settlements. They herded the Indian slaves into the mine, and then they used their mules to pull out the supporting timbers collapsing the front entrance to the mine. By that action, they had effectively murdered all the Indians they had captured and enslaved. They also concealed the entrance to the gold mine.

They immediately broke camp to head south for Mora. They saddled the horses and loaded up the camp supplies. They were getting out of these mountains before the Indians killed them all. They believed at least fifty and possibly a hundred Indians were involved in the attacks against them. They packed the remaining horses with all the gold and silver they could carry. The miners had lost eleven men and had five wounded men to slow them down.

When the pack train moved out two hours later, the strongest men were in front as they wanted to travel as fast and as far away from these savage Indians as possible. The wounded men were in the middle and the rear of the pack train of gold on the pack animals. As the day wore on and the wounded lagged behind, they found it was payback time from the Cheyenne. The Cheyenne warriors wanted revenge. They quickly killed any Spaniards or Frenchmen whom lagged behind. With two additional ambushes by Cheyenne warriors along the trails that day the Spanish and French had another seven men killed. The men who were wounded, and simply could not keep up with the rapid pace, disappeared and were never seen again after they lagged behind the main party of miners. None of the French or Spanish would slow up for their wounded friends. It became a disorderly flight, with each man for himself.

When the Spanish and French miners made camp that night, fear could be felt by all. Each man wondered if he would get out of this wilderness alive. There had been fifty-four French and Spanish men at the start of this summer. Now suddenly twenty-three had been killed in the heavy fighting with the Cheyenne warriors. Only thirty one were still alive at the end of the day. The Cheyenne had suffered heavier losses. Thirty-five men, women, and children were slaughtered in the mine when the Spanish and Frenchmen forced the Indians slaves into the mines then deliberately collapsed the mine down on top of them. Another warrior died in the dawn raid on the camp; so the Indian losses were thirty-six dead.

In the morning it was discovered that two more guards had been killed in the night. Normally the Cheyenne would not fight in the night; but they were out to get even for the murder of their families. The two sentries were too tempting of a target to pass up. The Cheyenne simply crawled in close and finished off the sentries with two arrows into each guard. Then the Indians stripped the dead of their rifles, gun powder and shot, along with their knives. The Cheyenne planned to return the shot (lead balls) back to their enemies!

With the arrival of dawn, the Spanish and French miners discovered two more men had been killed by Cheyenne warriors during the night. They had a cold breakfast of water and jerky, then saddled their horses and pack horses, loaded their gold and silver and took off headed south.

The spirits of twenty-five Spanish and French miners who had been killed by the Cheyenne also traveled along beside their companions.

They did not want anyone getting their share of the gold. But the twenty- nine Spanish and French miners did not see the twenty- five spirits or ghosts traveling alongside them. The spirits talked to each other as they could easily see each other. The miners who were still alive only talked with each other as they did not see the spirits of the men killed in battle.

As the pack train traveled south past Big Costilla Peak, the men knew that they were going to make it. The miners were about seventy to eighty miles north of their destination, the settlement at Mora. They could be there in four days while riding very carefully, on alert for any Cheyenne warriors. Of course they were not headed straight for Mora. They were circling around Mora to the west where they would cache the gold and silver away from anyone who would try and steal it from them. They would take two additional days to reach the safety of the settlement at Mora. Yes, things were already looking better. As the lands opened up with a lot of clear meadows, the Cheyenne Indians were now gone. They stopped to kill an elk and cook it over a campfire. The fire and the hot meal really can make a man feel better.

As the land had flattened out, and there were numerous meadows, and the lack of cover prevented the Cheyenne warriors from carrying out any attacks without a heavy loss of life. The Cheyenne warriors had been following their enemies long enough that they knew they were headed to the settlement of Mora. So they decided to circle around to the south and get ahead of their enemies. The Cheyenne warriors planned to set an ambush, two days travel ahead in the narrow canyons along Coyote Creek. By leaving the miners who had enslaved and murdered their families alone for two days they would relax their guard a little. It would also serve the Cheyenne warriors well as they could circle around ahead of their enemies and set their ambush into place. The Cheyenne warriors needed to get in close to effectively use bows and arrows to carry out the deadly ambush. Two days would also give them time to make a lot of arrows that they could use to kill their enemies.

Two days later the pack train came to the narrow canyon that Coyote Creek flows through on the way to Mora. As Spaniards saw the site, they just wanted to push on through. The French having trapped and fought Indians in the Rocky Mountains recognized a good site for an ambush. So the Frenchmen dropped back, casually offering to handle the pack animals. They told the Spaniards they would give them a hand with the pack animals in the narrow canyon. Their intent was to let the Spaniards locate the ambush first, and suffer the first causalities. The Frenchmen wanted to be in the center of the pack animals so that the animals would stop any arrows intended to kill them! They grabbed a pack animal and positioned one on the left and one on the right, and had the riding mount just behind them. They wanted to present to the Cheyenne as small of target as possible to shoot at.

When the first arrows slammed into the Spaniards, knocking them off their horses and to the ground, the Frenchmen realized they were correct about the ambush. After all it was only right that they let the Spaniards ride unaware into the ambush. The Spaniards just had to raid that last Cheyenne camp to get more slaves to mine gold. They did not wait for the Frenchmen to insure that they had killed or enslaved every Indian in the camp. Since the French did not trust the Spaniards, it only made common sense to let the Indians kill more of their partners so there was more gold for them. They could not be blamed for any of the Spaniards the Indians killed. They had nothing to do with it!

The Cheyenne waited until the enemy was fully into their ambush when they sprung the trap. For six minutes, until the pack train had fought its way clear of the ambush, that the Cheyenne held the advantage in the battle. The Cheyenne were able to kill five of the enemy with the loss of another warrior. They were most effective in killing the Spanish as they rode right into the trap. They were only able to kill one Frenchman and some pack animals because the Frenchmen had positioned themselves behind the pack animals, using them for cover.

After the battle, the Cheyenne were able to collect the weapons of the dead. They hoped to be able to use the two rifles they recovered against the men who had used these same weapons to attack their Indian encampment. They now had four working muzzle loading rifles. Unfortunately there was not much gun powder. There was only enough gunpowder to fire about three shots from each rifle. The Cheyenne who was most familiar with the black powder rifles showed three other warriors how to carefully load and aim the rifle. With only twelve shots available they had to make every shot count. The eldest warrior only let his companions fire one shot each to get familiar with the rifle and to see where the bullet hit on the target. He made it very clear that they were to save two shots each for the final battle where he wanted to kill these invaders in a final ambush.

Three days later on the mountain which came to be known as Sierra de los Brujos, the Spanish and Frenchmen arrived at their cache site on top of a mountain that was one days ride out of Mora. Here they began unloading the gold and silver ore. On top of the mountain, they had dug a tunnel underground leading in two directions. One tunnel was wide and high and had torches positioned along the tunnel wall to light the way to a treasure chest. What was in the second tunnel where they had piled old mining timbers they would not speak of.

The Spanish and French men could not believe their luck. They had been able to fight off the Cheyenne Indians these last two days. They had been so successful that not once had the Indians been able to get within the range where they could use their bow and arrows. Apparently the Cheyenne were too stupid to have grabbed up the powder horns with the gunpowder. They had lost four rifles, and there had been only four shots fired at them, off in the distance, the first day after the massacre on Coyote Creek. Obviously the Cheyenne did not know how to load the rifles or use the gunpowder. Yes, they had been lucky. Once they got the gold and silver into their underground cache all they had to do was activate the four traps and then fill in the hole around the tunnel into the cache site.

Everything was going well. They had loaded the gold and silver bars into the treasure room. They activated the traps by removing the timbers which held the death traps from moving or tripping. Then they began the process of filling in the hole. They would throw in the loose dirt, pour water on top, and then pack it down with a heavy stone. Next they shoveled in more dirt, added the water, and packed it down more as they proceeded to fill up the hole to the cache site.

The Cheyenne warriors observed the crazy French and Spaniards hauling the heavy metal rocks all the way from Colorado down here to the mountain by Mora, New Mexico.

Then they buried the heavy yellow rocks right back in the ground and filled in the hole in the ground. Why did they slaughter their families just for rocks? The Cheyenne warriors observed the Spanish and French men divide their group into two parts. One part was filling in the hole while the second group took the pack animals down to get water from the stream below at the base of the mountain. Then they dumped this water into the hole that they were filling in. In watching them carefully, they observed that the group getting water would be the easier group to ambush.

While the ten Cheyenne warriors were outnumbered, they simply waited until the intruders let their guard down or gave them an opening, and then they would attack. Then the Indians would withdraw until they could ambush them again.

And so it was up on the mountain that as one group of men filled in the hole in the ground; the second group took the pack animals to bring up water from the stream running down below the mountain. This water was poured on the soil as they tamped it down and compacted the ground as they filled in the hole leading into their cache site. Two hundred yards below the hole on the north slope was where the ambush was placed.

As the men returned with the final load of water that they used to pack the dirt down tightly, the men's thoughts had turned to the ride to Mora. When the ambush commenced, the French and Spanish miners were caught by complete surprise. The Cheyenne began their ambush by firing their rifles into the men returning with the pack train of water. The Cheyenne then set down the rifles and used the bows as they could aim and fire three arrows in the time it took to reload the black powder rifles. While the miners had tried to be careful; the ambush caught three men out in the open, and they died as the rifle bullets slammed into them. Then the arrows had wounded another three men.

When the men at the tunnel heard their companions coming under attack, six of them immediately grabbed their rifles and raced to help their companions. They ran headlong into the second ambush that the Cheyenne had set in place. The Cheyenne had placed five warriors to take advantage of the men running from camp without cover. When they were without protective cover, the Indians opened fire at close range, where their arrows were most effective. Three of the Spanish and French men were killed instantly while two more were wounded with the arrows. The Spanish and French miners quickly fell back to their camp. After firing their arrows, as the men returned to the camp on top of the mountain, the Cheyenne withdrew to observe the enemy and plan another ambush.

Now the Spanish and French miners wanted to get the hell out of there. In minutes, another six of their companions had died, and five more men were not much good in a fight since they were wounded. They had half their men standing guard, while the remainder of the unwounded men finished filling in the hole. Then they dry stacked rocks over the entrance to the tunnel.

Sixteen men rode with rifles in hand for Mora. Five of these men were wounded. Two of the wounded would die when they fell behind and the Cheyenne caught up with them on their way to the safety of the Spanish settlement.

When the men rode out for Mora, thirty eight spirits of the Spanish and French miners stayed at the cache site. Twenty of the spirits were Spanish, eighteen spirits were Frenchmen. They had worked and murdered to get this gold and silver and they were not going to let it out of their sight. The Spirits did not have the ability to move a single bar of bullion. They could not buy the house or lands that they had dreamed about when they returned to France or Spain. They would not see their old friends nor would they enjoy nice clothes or meals in the land they had planned to return to. They would not have that pretty wife they dreamed about. They were dead. They were now spirits or ghosts as some would call them. They stayed on the mountain with their cache of gold and silver bullion and they did their best to scare away people who would come up the mountain. In time the mountain would be called: Sierra de los Brujos or Mountain of the Witches.

★★The present time★★

Their reputation had kept them safe for over two centuries. Then they saw the two teenage girls. The French miners' spirits knew they could not scare the girls! Their defenses which had stood the test of time, people's fear of witches, and ghosts, collapsed with the arrival of the teenage girls! They knew that they could try and scare the girls—

and the Spanish spirits were prepared to try. But the French spirits told them that they always fowl things up! What happens after you try and scare the teenage girls and you fail? Those two girls will simply follow you back to our cache site—that is what they will do! The Frenchmen told the Spaniards that your stupidity will lead them to us again! The French pointed out that for now the best defense was to do nothing. Maybe the teenagers would give up or lose the trail. If they found the entrance then there were the Death Traps that the Spanish had built to kill the teenage girls.

While Dancing Wind and Molly O'Brien occasionally lost the trail they soon would realize their mistake and correct it. In a short time, they were back on the trail again. Once they walked by the cache site missing it by only a hundred yards. Then they started down the slope. The Frenchmen told the Spanish spirits, "See, we told you. They missed us! "But then the two teenage girls climbed back up the hill, to again pick up the trail.

In six days, the girls had worked out the trail. They arrived at the entrance to the cache site. The Spanish and French spirits / ghost came out of the tunnel where they were guarding their treasure to try and scare the two girls away, but they did not feel that they did a very good job scaring them when the two girls took off their backpacks and stopped to count the thirty eight spirits. The two women changed angles to ensure that they counted every spirit because there were so many spirits clustered over the entrance to the cache site. All the spirits realized that while the women could clearly see them; when they had casually removed their backpacks and pointed with their finger as they counted each spirit it simply was not the behavior of a frightened individual! The thirty eight spirits knew that their reputation as witches had collapsed when the girls did not run away! In fact the two teenagers recognized them as gold and silver miners who were killed by the Cheyenne Indians after they had slaughtered and enslaved the peaceful Cheyenne Indians. Finally, Molly O'Brien and Dancing Wind stopped to discuss the dry stacked rocks.

Over the centuries they had grown a lush growth of green moss. Molly asked Dancing Wind if it was the air flowing in and out of the tunnels which caused the growth of moss.

Dancing Wind did not know. The Angel to Dancing Wind's right told her no; she thought the green moss was actively grown by the spirits living in the tunnel to camouflage the site. The Angel went on to explain that the site was made about 1700-1750. To ensure that the two girls were aware of the danger in the tunnels the Angel told them about the four death traps placed there when the site was built. The Angel also suggested that they look for a back door mostly in a north to northwest direction which would enable the girls to avoid the Death Traps. The Guardian Angels told them the choice was theirs. It was up to Dancing Wind and Molly—did they want to enter the stone door and go inside the tunnels at the top of Sierra de los Brujos?

Then it started raining. The Rain Spirits did what the thirty-eight Spanish and French spirits were unable to do. The two teenagers left the mountain to get out of the rain and get into warm dry clothes. For thirty days, occasionally heavy rains occurred on the Mountain of the Witches. Then after two weeks of dry sunny weather which allowed the roads to dry out, the spirits saw the return of the two teenage trackers. Up the bumpy dirt road, they saw the teenagers coming in an old pickup truck piled high with camping and mining equipment and supplies. Certainly the spirits did not like the persistence these teenage girls showed.

Arriving close to the secret tunnels the two teenagers set up a camp. Then they walked over to the entrance to the tunnel where the spirits argued inside. While the spirits argued about whose fault it was that the teenagers had been able to find them, the two girls got down to work.

Dancing Wind and Molly were dressed in their work clothes: heavy jeans and long flannel shirts with work gloves and shovels, picks, rakes, and steel digging bars. While Dancing Wind used the rake to pull the green, moss colored rocks off the pile and drag them five feet away. Molly picked up and stacked the rocks in a pile another ten feet further away.

After working about seven minutes, Molly saw Dancing Wind retreat away from the pile of rocks as a four foot long rattle snake emerged from under the pile of rocks. Molly grabbed a shovel and scooped up the rattle snake and moved the snake over fifty feet from where they were working. Removing the rattle snakes from the rocks occurred twice as the woman removed all the rocks piled over where they intended to dig a hole to enter the entrance to the cache site. Because the teenagers' Guardian Angels warned them about the snakes that might be found in the pile of rocks, the teenagers did not pick up the rocks directly from the pile but used the five foot rake to dislodge the rocks and pull them off the pile. By day's end, the trackers had cleared a fifteen foot circle around the entrance so they had a clear working area to start digging in the morning.

After a big breakfast of eggs, sausage and toast made in the skillet, the two girls walked over to their site to begin the hard backbreaking work of using the pick, shovel and digging bar to dig the hole. It was hard packed ground and the teenagers had only been able to dig three feet in four hours! At one in the afternoon, they broke for lunch. Then they returned after lunch to attack the hard packed soil pushing their hole deeper and deeper. Slowly the hard packed soil and rocks gave way to their persistent effort. By three thirty they and had dug four feet. They stopped for a thirty minute break; and when they returned to the hole, they carried they with them a ten foot aluminum step ladder that they got out of the bed of the pickup truck. The ladder was needed to help them climb in and out of the hole. By working hard and regularly trading places in the hole as each became exhausted, they were able to dig another two feet in the afternoon. In ten hours of work they had dug a hole five feet deep. The teenagers called it a day.

Around the campfire that night they ate their dinner and discussed their days work and their plans for tomorrow. They hoped to find a stone door tomorrow; yes that would make their day. After the fire burned low, they poured water on the fire to put it out. The exhausted girls crawled into their tent and were soon fast asleep.

Morning sunrise found the teenagers getting up to fix breakfast and each of them explained that they had done the most work yesterday as they had more sores and blisters to prove it. After a big breakfast, the hard work of digging began again. Digging bars were slammed into the earth to break up an inch of soil at a time. Sometimes the dirt flung out of the hole was caught by the playful Wind Spirits and sent right down into the digger's face, only to have to be shoveled up and thrown out of the hole again. The girl who was resting while the other girl dug was removing the shoveled dirt to a pile of dirt about six feet away from the hole so the soil would not suddenly cause the hole to cave in and bury the digger.

After two and a half hours of digging, at a depth of six feet, Dancing Wind smiled as she told Molly: "Hear that? It sounds hollow now when I slam the digging bar into the soil! "Molly told her come on out and let her dig awhile. After another two inches both agreed the hollow sound was getting louder. They stopped for a break to eat and drink then Dancing Wind started digging where the hollow sound was loudest. Slamming the digging bar into the soil and rocks, she worked them loose and then shoveled them out of the hole. Finally she stopped exhausted and climbed out of the hole. Molly resumed the digging and after thirty minutes she hit a flat rock which sounded hollow behind it. They traded places again and Dancing Wind enlarged the hole. The more the hole was enlarged, the clearer it became they were on top of a large flat stone.

By late afternoon, they had cleared around the stone and could clearly establish that it was a square cut stone set or recessed into a large square opening. They were excited because they now had their stone door! Now they began the task of trying to open the stone door. Try as they might they could not move the stone out of its recessed opening with pry bars as the stone was just too heavy for the two teenagers to move.

Next the two trackers tried their backup plan. From the bed of the pickup truck, the teenagers unloaded a steel tripod with a pulley at the top of it. This was set up over the top of the hole. Next, a hundred foot extension cord was run from the generator sitting in the bed of the pickup truck to the bottom of the hole.

In the bottom of the hole, Molly put a half inch rock cutting drill bit into her hammer drill, she put on a face mask to protect her from breathing the dust, placed safety goggles over her eyes, put hearing protection over her eyes, put on her gloves and then she began the assault against the immoveable stone door!

For fifteen minutes she drilled into the solid stone door cutting a half inch hole into the center of the door. When her hole was three inches deep, she stopped drilling. The generator was shut off, and the hammer drill put back into the truck. Next Dancing Wind removed a box of nitrile gloves, a two part epoxy, and a steel anchor bolt from the truck and took them over to Molly who was still down in the hole. Molly blew all the rock dust out of the hole she had drilled into the stone door. Then she put on the nitrile gloves and sat down and mixed up the epoxy and poured it all down into the hole. Then she pushed down into the epoxy a half inch anchor bolt. Epoxy oozed out of the hole, but Molly did not mind; she just wanted to ensure the anchor bolt was completely surrounded by epoxy. Then they let the epoxy harden overnight.

In the morning both girls wanted to start trying to open the stone door immediately, but they realized that this would be a very long day for them so they began with a good solid breakfast. Today would be the longest and hardest day of all.

After breakfast, the tripod was checked, and lines were tied to adjoining trees to the top of the tripod to prevent any movement. Then a line was attached from the truck's bumper, through the pulley on the top of the tripod, down to the anchor bolt in the stone door. The truck would be used to pry open the stone door! The door that both women were unable to budge was slowly opened as Dancing Wind drove the truck forward six feet under Molly's guidance. Then the trucks wheels were blocked with rocks so the truck could not move. Then the stone door was secured with more ropes so it too would not move.

Next, Molly and Dancing Wind got a silver dollar out of the cab of the truck. They would flip a coin to see who would enter the stone door; and journey where no man or woman had traveled for centuries. Whoever lost the coin toss would remain outside the door on top of the ground and be the safety belayer for the climbing ropes the one entering the stone door would use. The coin toss was won by Molly, so Dancing Wind would be her sole back up should she run into problems.

Together they went over the pack Molly would wear. In her back pack she carried food and water, climbing gear (carabiners, pursik's, rock anchors, hammer) first aid kit, spare batteries, spare flashlight, spare walkie-talkie, a knife, hand gun, spare ammo, spare gloves, a duffel bag , spare rope, and a star drill. She would wear a climbing harness with the climbing rope secure to her and slowly fed to her as needed from above. In her hand she would descend through the door with a spotlight and walkie-talkie tied to her left hand. Another spot light would dangle below her as she descended through the opening.

As Molly descended twenty feet into the hole, her flood light touched the stone floor first. When she reached the bottom of the shaft she immediately told Dancing Wind that she was in. Then she set up the first spot light to shine down the stone passage way. In the distance she thought she could just make out a large treasure chest about seventy feet down the wide passage way. Before moving a foot she let Dancing Wind know what she had found. Before moving a step she would discuss every action and get joint agreement on whatever action she would take.

Along the passageway, the French and Spanish spirits watched the events unfold. The French spirits were along the first twenty feet of the passage way, while the Spanish spirits were watching from two locations in the tunnel and beside the treasure chest. The Frenchmen's spirits were not too happy about what the Spanish spirits had planned for the unsuspecting teenage girls, but they, like many bystanders in life, would not make any effort to help the teenagers stay alive! They would make no effort to warn them of the danger nor try to assist them in any way!

Slowly and carefully Molly traveled down the stone corridor towards the treasure chest. She talked to Dancing Wind each foot of the way on their walkie-talkies. Before moving a foot, she carefully and slowly examined the tunnel walls, roof, and floor looking for a death trap.

Along the tunnel the miners' spirits were anxiously watching the progress of the teenage girl. The Spaniards who had built the death traps centuries ago knew that shortly they would be activated by the teenager's weight passing down the corridor or her greed as she grabbed the treasure chest. A couple of the French spirits were cynical about how effective the death traps would be. They had a nagging feeling in the back of their minds that these were not ordinary teenagers. Certainly no normal teenagers could have found their hiding spot and opened the stone door.

At twenty feet down the stone passage way, Molly told Dancing Wind over the two way radio, about the passageway on her left. Her initial glance at the alcove told her it seemed to only go about seven feet then end. This dead end room seemed to be just a storage area for large timbers used to support the shaft or used in mining. So she moved on down the passageway towards the treasure chest she could see in her spotlight fifty feet further down the tunnel.

Molly picked up her pace. She wanted to get to the treasure. Suddenly she felt the floor start to give way and settle under her weight. She pivoted and dove backwards as far as she could as the roar of falling rocks slammed down beside her! Dancing Wind screamed over the radio: "Molly are you all right? Molly are you all right? "Molly replied, "I'm okay but I just had a close call." The floor trap was activated by the weight of a man walking down the corridor. This trap dropped a series of five, one hundred pound rocks onto the heads of anyone walking down the corridor. Only by jumping backwards before the first stone crashed down from the ceiling had Molly avoided the trap. Before moving on, Molly carefully studied the ceiling and walls around the trap. There on the walls high up, just inches down from the ceiling were the warning signs she was looking for and had failed to see. There on the wall chiseled into the stone were two lightning bolts. One was on the right side of the walls, and one was on the left--two eight inch long lightning bolts! The warning sign for the death traps was a lightning bolt engraved in the walls just below the ceiling.

Another twenty feet down the tunnel she spotted another pair of lightning bolts on the ceiling. This time she knew that there was a trap.

Unfortunately she could not see the location on the ceiling where the trap fell down on top of her head. She called Dancing Wind about the lightning bolts and asked her for her ideas. Dancing Wind suggested she get five feet of slack in her safety line—then take a running jump and jump over the ceiling trap trigger. Even though neither teenager could see the trap they both realized that there was another trap before they reached the treasure chest.

On top of the hole, Dancing Wind had fed out five feet of line to Molly down below. Molly backed up four feet and took a running jump to jump over the Spanish ceiling trap.

The instant her feet landed she knew something was going terribly wrong behind her, the floor tipped skyward as the floor gave way under her feet! As the floor opened up there in front of her face and below her feet a black abyss was opening up, and she was powerless to stop her slide into the black pit below! She let out a terrified scream as she began sliding into the black pit opening before her.

On top of the ground Dancing Wind heard the terrified scream, then moments later the shock hit her as the rope bit into her skin as Molly's entire weight slammed into the dynamic belay that Dancing Wind used to secure Molly's safety with the climbing ropes.

Down in the tunnel Molly's feet hung over the black abyss wanting to swallow her up. But for the climbing rope securing her to Dancing Wind; she would have fallen to her death in the black pit below her. Slowly Molly realized she was not going anywhere; she got on the radio and let Dancing Wind know what had happened. Had the search light and walkie-talkie not been tied to her body, both would have fallen into the dark pit she dangled over. This second trap was a pivoting stone in the floor dropping one into a thirty foot deep pit. Once the trap was sprung, and it had dropped the men into the trap below; which was designed to break the intruders arms and legs in the fall; the pivoting stone reset itself. The trap was then ready to kill the next group of people traveling down the tunnel. The floor trap was also activated by the weight of a man walking down the corridor. The floor had pivoted to drop her into the pit below, but she did not fall as the safety line to her climbing harness had stopped her fall. Her feet were in the air and her face was about six inches above the floor. As she looked for a way out she noticed the lightning bolts about six inches above the floor. These lightning bolts were just above the floor instead of just below the ceiling as on the last trap. Slowly she inched her way back up the line and suddenly as the center of gravity shifted the stone floor pivoted and resumed its normal position. The floor looked completely normal. Molly then let Dancing Wind know she was safe, and this time before she crossed the floor trap she walked back to the small room where the timbers were stored. She took six of the timbers and laid them across the floor trap so she had a safe bridge across the trap.

Her progress down the tunnel was even slower now. But soon she arrived at the treasure chest. She had traveled through seventy feet of tunnel and survived two death traps to reach the treasure chest. As she looked inside the treasure chest, she saw the kind of rich gold ore miner's dream of finding. If she loaded up her back pack with this high grade gold ore she would be able to sell it for thousands of dollars.

Now this time, instead of acting on impulse, she stopped to get guidance from her Guardian Angel. She wanted to get her Guardian Angel's opinion as she might see a danger Molly had failed to see. The Angel started by asking a question, *"How many traps did I tell you were guarding the treasure? "*Molly stopped for a moment to think back upon their discussion and then she remembered that the Angel told her that there are four death traps. Next the Angel asked her, *"How many death traps have you encountered?"* Molly replied, "Two." So her Guardian Angel asked Molly: *"So how many death traps are still guarding the treasure? "*Molly knew that there were still two traps protecting the treasure.

Molly turned to the Angel and asked her then is this treasure chest a death trap?

The Angel replied, *"Of course it is a death trap. When you go to grab the bait which is this treasure chest, the ceiling will collapse down upon the treasure chest killing them. This is simply the third death trap!"*

So Molly called Dancing Wind and told her what the Angel had told her. Dancing Wind told Molly let it go. It is not worth risking your life for $10,000 in gold. Molly told Dancing Wind and her Guardian Angel, "NO! I am not walking away from $10,000. It is just sitting there right in front of me. In ten minutes, I can get us $10,000 and I simply cannot walk away from that kind of money after all the work I did! So realizing how stubborn Molly could be at times Dancing Wind suggested that if it is a trap; instead of bending over the treasure chest and taking the rich high grade gold ore from it, instead, in case it is a trap, tie a line to the treasure chest and drag it to the stone door. Molly agreed. She tied a line around the iron handles of the wooden treasure chest and then the other end of the ten foot length of rope; she started to tie around her waist. Suddenly she heard her Guardian Angel telling her instead of tying the rope around her waist, pull with the rope in your hands instead, that way if you suddenly decide you do not want the treasure or the treasure chest anymore, you can let go if you decide to run or leave the trap in a hurry. So instead of Molly tying the rope around her waist she held the rope in her hands as she took off pulling her treasure chest towards the entrance to the tunnel.

Almost instantly, there was a loud roar at the back of the tunnel, the ceiling collapsed down on top of the treasure chest burying it, and the surrounding area in twenty tons of stone. As the roar of falling rocks gained momentum, Molly dropped her rope and took off running for the tunnel entrance, but was overtaken by a fast moving cloud of dust and dirt which blocked out all visibility. Dancing Wind screamed out her dear friends name as she heard the roar of falling rocks. Then a dark cloud of dust poured out the tunnel entrance. Moments later Molly emerged from the cloud of dust. Molly climbed out of the hole and both teenagers decided they needed a rest and a break.

Over some hot mint tea, the teenagers discussed the tunnel, what they saw and the advice the Angels had given. Dancing Wind thought about what was said and then told Molly the real treasure room must be down the dead end tunnel where the old timbers are stored. So after a half hour break, Molly returned to the tunnel to explore the short dead end tunnel where the heavy timbers were stored.

When Molly walked into the little room, as she approached the back wall, she noticed that instead of ending as she had first thought, the tunnel made a ninety degree left hand turn. As Molly walked down the tunnel carefully looking for any lightning bolts near the ceiling or floor, she also turned to the right and looked at the Angel beside her for any suggestions. The Angel just said: *"You are doing okay so far but don't drop your guard; there is still one trap in front of you!"*

Molly carefully searched the walls, floor, and ceiling as she moved down the stone tunnel, suddenly it took a right hand turn and there before her was a treasure room filled with brilliant gold bars of bullion and bars of silver which had turned black over the years of storage. Molly started to step forward, but her Guardian Angel stretched out her hand blocking her path.

Molly looked at the Angel for two minutes but could not detect anything but love in her actions of blocking her path into the treasure room where tons of precious metal was stored. So Molly turned away from the Angel and used her search light to study the walls for the lightning bolts; but there were none! So Molly looked harder to find any indications of a trap. There over the ceiling; centered above the entrance way was a tiny four inch red lightning bolt. There was one more death trap protecting the treasure room.

So Molly turned to her Guardian Angel for advice. Her Guardian Angel told her: *"Do not let greed here get you killed! The spirits of the dead Frenchmen and Spaniards originally wanted four bars of gold each. But they got greedy and their subsequent actions resulted in their deaths. Why don't you give them something to think about? Just take four bars of gold for each of you. Leave the rest to show the spirits and the Angels watching that you are not affected by greed. Certainly you will leave the French and Spanish miners something to think about."* When Molly agreed and then told Dancing Wind her plans; Molly turned to the Angel and asked her, "What should I do? "The Angel told Molly, *"Just follow my actions exactly."*

Then the Angel pretended to open the duffel bag in the corridor outside the treasure room. So Molly opened the duffel bag in the corridor outside the treasure room. Then the Angel walked into the center of the room where a pile of gold bars were stacked. The Angel pretended to pick up the gold bar and carry it out of the treasure room and place it in the duffel bag. So Molly went to the exact bar of gold and grabbed it and started for the duffel bag; as soon as it had cleared the pile, it crashed to the floor as it was too heavy for Molly to carry! Lifting one end of the gold bar she had to drag it to the duffel bag and after slipping the gold bar into the duffel bag she dragged the bag to where she had entered the stone door; and placed the gold bar at the tunnel entrance. Then she returned to the gold room with the Angel.

Instead of grabbing another gold bar from the same location, the Guardian Angel surprised Molly by selecting a gold bar from the opposite side of the pile of gold bullion. Molly followed the Angel's guidance and after pushing the gold bar off the pile, and it again crashing to the floor she lifted one end of the gold bar and dragged it to the corridor outside the room where she again got it into the duffel bag which she dragged over to the entrance. One at a time, the Angel pretended to take a gold bar from opposite sides of the pile of gold bars going cattycorner around the pile of gold like one tightens lug nuts on a car tire until eight gold bars had been dragged to the entrance of the ancient cache. Molly and Dancing Wind thanked the Angel for her counsel.

Up the ladder, Molly climbed to pull on a rope with Dancing Wind. Using the try pod with the pulleys they had placed above their opening into the ancient chamber they pulled up the gold bars one by one until all eight bars of gold were outside the ancient depository. Then the safety ropes securing the stone door in place were removed and Molly guided Dancing Wind as she backed up the truck and the stone door was returned into place. Then both women grabbed gloves and shovels filing in the hole concealing the ancient stone door. Then the hole was filled in. Leaves, brush and rocks were scattered over the site so no trace of their digging remained.

One gold bar at a time was placed in the duffel bag, and each teenager grabbed a handle to carry the duffel bag up to the pickup truck. In thirty minutes all eight bars were safely loaded into the tool box in the bed of the truck. All their mining supplies and camping gear was then collected and placed into the truck bed as the sun set in the western sky.

As the two exhausted teenage trackers wearily climbed into the cab of the pickup truck

They smiled and gave each other a hug. It had been a very long day and they desperately wanted a hot shower. Dancing Wind suggested they get a steak dinner at the Cattle Rustler's Steak House. They started the truck and began driving off the Mountain of the Witches. As darkness descended upon the mountain they felt the evening wind on their faces and they heard the owls hooting to each other.

Sierra de los Brujos is the name the old Spanish people call the

Mountain of the Witches. Here on this mountain, change was slow to come. But change did come with the arrival of the two teenage girls who tracked the old trails. The night wind spoke of the changes and the owls spoke of the changes and watched the events unfold. Even the Angels were happy with the lessons that their charges had learned upon the mountain. As one French ghost saw the two teenagers drive off, he turned and said to the ghosts of the other French miners and trappers beside him, *"I sure would be proud to have a daughter like either one of those teenagers."* The Guardian Angel's riding in the back of the bed of the pickup truck overheard what the French ghost had said and the comment had put a big smile on both the teenagers' and the Guardian Angel's faces.

Angels are Small
And Angels are Tall
Angels bring Messages
Of GOD's Love to All

The Thief Who Robbed a House and Stole *Trust*

O nce upon a time, as fairy tales often start, there lived a father, mother, daughter and son in a house in the old southwest, northwest, southeast, or northeast, or wherever you are reading this story at. You see, there are sons and daughters like this everywhere.

While Dancing Wind and her good friend Molly were off tracking, and her father and mother were out shopping, a thief slipped into their home. The thief systematically searched the house from top to bottom. There was no drawer left that hadn't been searched. The mattresses were even checked under by the thief. The night stands were searched. If there was a dresser drawer it was tossed. Every box in the closet, both high and low was ransacked. But the thief did not take the walkie-talkies. Nor was the tiny portable color television, still unwrapped in the shopping bag taken! The thief did not touch the check books or the credit cards! Nor did the thief have any interest in the mother's favorite dolls, as these were not taken! The thief who came to rob the house was not interested in taking the son's hunting rifle! The thief went through the first aid kits and yet he did not touch the antibiotics, nor were the syringes to inject his mother's medicine taken. The thief it seems, only wanted money! Before leaving the house the thief went into his parent's bedroom and opened the bedroom windows and pushed out the screen. Now anyone who looked could see the thief entered by the window. Then the thief went out the front door, the same way he had entered, and locked it!

When the husband and wife returned they saw that the house had been thrown and called the police to report the robbery. Both the husband and wife were mad that their house had been ransacked and robbed. They both felt as if the thief had physically violated them!

Finally when they could stay awake no longer they went to bed. The window screen flapped in the wind. When the window screen flapped against the house, the husband and wife awakened at the sound and thought the thief had returned again in the night. It was only the wind hitting the window screen against the window frame and the exterior wall of the house, and crying out its warning to the husband and wife.

In the morning Dancing Wind's father went out and tried to put the window screen back in place, but the window screen refused to go back into place. As the father tried to reinstall the window screen he wondered who burglarized their home.

The Angel who leaned against the outside wall of the house turned to Dancing Wind's dad and asked: *"How did the thief get in the house? "*

Her dad replied, "First the thief used a knife to remove the screen. Then the man used the knife to slide between the window frames between the two glass panes and push up on the latch to open the window."

The Angel said, *"Oh, really? Then why could you not put the window screen back in place? What is holding the metal screen frame to the window frame? "*

The dad told the angel, "What holds the window screen to the window frame is simply soft caulking."

"Really? Soft caulking would easily be cut by a knife. Why was the soft caulking still intact? "

He knew the answer was no knife had been used to force open the window screen!

The Angel continued, *"Then why are there no knife scratches on the latch? "*

"Because the thief did not use a knife to open the window."

"If you look at the broken glass window and the numerous piles of broken glass inside the house, where did the force applied to the glass come from? "

"Outside the house. The force is directed inward."

"If most of the glass is clearly outside of the house then where was the person applying the force to break the glass? "

"He was inside the house when he broke the window! The force is directed outward."

"What was the position of the person who broke your windows and then forced out the screens? "(The broken glass was out in the yard, so the window was broken from inside the bedroom, the thief was inside the house when he broke the windows to show someone broke in)

The man said nothing, because he knew the answer to the Angel's questions.

His wife confided in her husband, "I no longer felt safe in the house! I feel violated, with someone going through my clothes. I am not safe here anymore! "The man did not know what to say. He did not want to hurt his wife more! When the thief had come and robbed the house; what that thief stole was TRUST!

Life is not always easy
For it is only by overcoming
Life's obstacles that you can grow
So do not be discouraged by setbacks
For they are intended to help you grow

The Last Days of Miguel Valdez and Maria Velasquez

In the fall, after the harvest of crops and the shearing of sheep, families got together in Socorro, New Mexico to celebrate the fiestas. Here Miguel Valdez met Maria Velasquez. Miguel was a hard working farmer who cultivated his dad's irrigated land. Miguel was a sixteen year old teenager and when he saw Maria he knew she was the woman he wanted for his wife. Maria also wanted a good hard working husband. After all, she was fourteen, and it was time she found a husband. She was looking for a handsome and hard working man who could support her. She thought Miguel would be a good choice as many times she had seen him helping his father with irrigating the land where they grew corn, pinto beans, and chili. It was an added bonus to her that Miguel was very strong and handsome.

Miguel told his dad, Juan, that he wanted to have Maria Velasquez as his wife and would he be willing to talk with Maria's dad Alfonso about his marrying his daughter. In Spanish families in the 1800's, marriages were arranged through the families.

It seems that what should have been a simple matter as far as Miguel and Maria were concerned suddenly became a lot more complicated once their parents blessings and permission were asked for. Alfonso Velasquez felt that anyone who really wanted to marry his daughter Maria should be a man of means and able to provide for her. Alfonso Velasquez said that anyone who wanted to marry his Maria must have two hundred dollars! Then the prospective husband could give Alfonso one hundred dollars, and Alfonso would give his permission for the wedding! Alfonso would also give Maria and her husband ten acres of irrigated land to build their adobe house on and farm. Alfonso said that the irrigated land was very fairly priced at ten dollars an acre. If a man who wanted to marry his daughter really was serious about the marriage then he must have $200!

Miguel was stunned. He had never had ten dollars in his life! Where was he to get two hundred dollars? Maria was in despair, how was she ever to find a husband if the husband she married had to have two hundred dollars? Never had Maria seen so much money in her life. Maria knew her dad wanted the best for her; but where could Miguel get that much money? Two hundred dollars was an impossible sum of money!

Miguel and Maria discussed how to raise two hundred dollars. The plan that they finally agreed upon was that during the spring, Miguel would help his father with the farming. Then in the summer Juan Valdez would lend his son Miguel a horse after the plowing and planting had been done. Miguel could take the horse and use it to prospect for the summer. If he could find a placer gold deposit then possibly in a month he might make the two hundred dollars. The merchants in Socorro would give him ten dollars an ounce for the placer gold. The Socorro merchant would then turn around and get twenty dollars an ounce for the gold when they sold it. Miguel figured he would have to recover twenty ounces of gold if he wanted Maria Velasquez as his wife.

Maria told Miguel that she would also work to make as much money as she could. Since cash was very hard to get, in desperation she went to see Pueblo. Pueblo was not a nice man. Pueblo was a rich man who had many sheepherders working for him. Pueblo had a lot of sheep and he told Maria that if she agreed to work for him on his ranch for four years he would give Maria her choice of forty of his sheep. That was ten sheep a year. But if Maria did not stick to the agreement and work all four years then she got nothing!

To Pueblo, it was a simple business deal. Since Pueblo had no dignity, no honor, no sense of honesty or fair play, nor any respect for women he intended to cheat Maria and pay her nothing! After all, a fourteen year old girl would not last four years tending sheep. She would probably work a couple of months and give up. Then Pueblo will have gotten a sheepherder to labor for him for free. Pueblo had to pay a sheepherder ten dollars a month. Let's see, that comes out to eighty dollars a year. Certainly Pueblo could not be expected to pay a sheepherder over the winter months. The sheepherder was lucky working for a rich man like Pueblo. Why Pueblo would give the sheepherder food for his camp while he tended the sheep. Pueblo would give them all the beans and flour and salt they needed to eat. If the sheepherder wanted more food or a greater variety of food he could pay for the extra food himself.

With Maria, Pueblo felt he was doing her a favor; everyone knows a woman cannot do work as hard or as good as a man. Yes, Pueblo was being more than fair giving her ten sheep a year. Why his sheep were worth three dollars each. Why that was thirty dollars! Who but a generous man like Pueblo would pay a woman thirty dollars a year? By hiring a woman, he could save the extra money he would have to pay a man. Instead of eighty dollars, he would pay a man for the same job he agreed to give Maria, thirty dollars. He would save fifty dollars the first year. Of course if Maria quit, she would not cost him one dollar.

The first year Juan prospected the mountains to the west of Socorro on the east side of the Rio Grande. Juan did a lot of riding and digging of holes but he found no gold. Juan had no experience prospecting for gold and he had selected a poor place to prospect. Naturally Juan had nothing to show for the summer's work.

When the summer ended Maria was very disappointed that Miguel had saved up no money at all. She thought I will never get a husband at this rate. She suggested to Miguel that next summer he go to Pinos Altos by Silver City and learn how to find gold from the gringo (white) prospectors. There were many stories about them finding gold. Miguel did not like the idea of working for the white miners but he wanted Maria for his wife so he finally agreed.

The second year found Maria still herding sheep for Pueblo. She figured it was very hard work but after four years she would have forty sheep to raise for wool and mutton on the ten acres Miguel would buy from her dad. In the fall when Miguel returned he was stronger and more handsome than ever. Maria was happy too that Miguel had managed to save seventy five dollars from his summer's work placer mining gold at Pinos Altos. Miguel was so happy to see Maria. All he could think about was having her for his wife. Never before had he ever held as much money, as he now had seventy five silver dollars.

He told Maria that he had learned to recognize the gravel which held the placer gold and many times he had shoveled the rich gravel into the sluice boxes. Now with a gold pan he could pan down the gravel in minutes and see if it held the gold he searched for. But he would never get ahead unless he had his own spot to mine gold, because the mine owners kept most of the gold and only gave the men working for them a small portion of the gold the workers recovered.

Very reluctantly Maria agreed that Miguel should take his father's horse and go prospecting for the third summer, since they had both been doing their best to save money for their marriage. Maria would return to herding sheep for Pueblo. For two years he had not paid Maria one penny! This would be Maria's third year working for Pueblo.

This summer Miguel worked the mountains east of Socorro. In a month of hard work, Miguel could say without a doubt that they contained no gold deposit that would pay wages. Then Miguel worked and prospected the mountains to the southwest of Socorro, the Chupadera Mountains. There were tiny specks of gold he found but not in any quantity that would pay him any wages. Miguel dry panned many washes and arroyos looking for a good placer deposit but there was none.

At the fall fiestas Miguel was disappointed, he had not found gold and had nothing to show for his summer of prospecting, but he told Maria he was a better prospector than ever, and he knew that given a little more time he felt sure he could make a gold strike. Maria told him about all the difficulty with Pueblo she was having. He was yelling at her and trying to get her to quit so he would not have to pay her the sheep he had agreed to. Maria said she would not quit until he paid her or gave her the sheep she was promised.

When the fourth summer came, Miguel was again off prospecting. This time he traveled much further to the southeast from Socorro at the Oscura Mountains; which are a little to the north and east of the north end of the Jornada Del Muerto (Journey of Death) Miguel's father suggested trying the higher more rugged mountains to locate a gold deposit. Miguel thought his idea of gold being located in the rugged mountains made sense and he agreed to follow his father's idea.

For three months, Miguel worked in the Oscura Mountains working his way from north to south carefully digging holes down to bedrock and panning the gravel for gold, but he found none. As he was filling his canvas water bag at a spring on the southeast side of the

Oscura Mountains, something higher up in the rocks seemed to catch and hold his attention. So he climbed up higher in the mountains and there he found a quartz contact zone between the barren igneous rocks. He collected four samples of the rocks and took them down to the spring. He used a larger sixty pound rock tied to a young green tree as a spring to lift the heavy stone.

In a hammering motion, he would use the force of his shoulders and arms to throw or force down the sixty pound stone to smash the quartz rock in a rhythmic motion with the stone rising and falling, crushing the quartz stones into a powder.

The powder from the crushed quartz was then placed in his gold pan and panned for gold. In a circular motion, water swirled around his gold pan. He would raise and lower one end of the pan washing out the lighter material. Occasionally he added more water, dipping the gold pan into the spring as he panned and washed the lighter material out of his pan. As he got down to the final remainder of his pan he said "Holy Mother of Mary! Thank You! " The bottom of Miguel's pan was covered in gold!

Miguel was a happy man as he fixed his dinner that night of beans. He also ate a little watercress he found growing in the spring. Tomorrow he would explore the quartz vein and see where it ran. He wanted to find the richest gold in the vein by sampling along the quartz vein. He planned to take up into the mountain with him his horse's saddle blanket so he could fold it up and use it like a sack to carry more gold ore down to the spring to crush and pan.

That night Miguel dreamed of bars of gold and his marriage to Maria. Yes, he told himself he would have eight boys with Maria. Well, maybe one girl also would be okay. Yes, they would have a grand adobe house with servants and he would have a stable of fine horses.

For two weeks Miguel worked fourteen and sixteen hour days

mining his gold. Then he took some dead dry juniper wood and broke it into small pieces and set it on fire. When the wood was burning nice and hot, he threw dirt on top of the fire smothering the fire. Miguel was doing his best to try and make charcoal. Then he made a bellows out of wood and his horse blanket. This he used, with the charcoal to make a very hot fire to heat the fine gold dust up to two thousand degrees so he could melt the fine gold dust. Using his bullet mold he then cast twenty one small gold nuggets. He hoped each round ball of gold weighed one ounce. He figured he had twenty one ounces of gold! Now he could go see Maria's father Alfonso Velasquez and establish his right to marry his daughter.

Miguel broke camp and started back to Socorro. Riding his horse he rounded the south end of the Oscura Mountains and moved north along the west side of mountain range. Yes, Miguel was in a good mood as he sang *La Marcha*, a Spanish wedding song. Late in the afternoon as he rode past one arroyo he had a prickly feeling along his back and it felt like the hair on his neck was standing up. Miguel looked back and saw nine Comanche warriors riding out of the arroyo he had just passed! "Aye Dios! " (Oh GOD!) He said. Then Miguel spurred his horse into a run to the northwest towards Socorro.

Behind Miguel the nine warriors kicked their horses into a run. Each Comanche wanted to be the one to capture the Spaniard, kill him and obtain his rifle and horse as a prize. The race was on and they rode their horses like the wind across the staked plains of New Mexico.

Neither the Spaniard nor the Comanche's expected the horse race to last long but it did. Through the evening and night the riders rode their horses doing their best to get all possible endurance and speed out of their mounts.

For Miguel, this was the scariest ride of his life. There were nine Comanche riding behind him. Effectively the Comanche had nine horses he had to outride while he had his dad's best farm horse. He tried to move with the horse to get all possible speed out of his horse. He wished he had been able to grain feed his horse as they can run father and faster than a horse just grazing on grass. He put all his thoughts and energy into making this the best ride of his life. He was badly scared about the torture he would receive at the hands of the Comanche should they capture him!

Miguel knew the end was near when he saw the blood spatters in the foam around the mouth of his father's favorite horse. He saw that his favorite horse was coughing up blood and he knew that his horse had given his life to try and save Miguel. Miguel's fear intensified as he knew he could not outfight the nine Comanche warriors.

As Miguel reached the foothills of the small mountains or hills, twenty miles to the southeast of Socorro, the end came quickly when his horse collapsed on the first hill. Within a minute the Comanche's had him. Miguel was tortured and killed on the small bell shaped hill.

Two weeks later Pueblo heard from one of his numerous sheepherders about Miguel's death to Indians. That gave Pueblo an idea. He had been furious that Maria intended to take her forty sheep next week. The more he had thought about it the madder he got. No woman was going to take his sheep. Why, forty sheep were worth $120 dollars! Maria told Pueblo that four years would be up next week and so she had completed her part of the agreement and would take forty of Pueblo's sheep as they had agreed. Now Pueblo thought, that is why she had started before shearing time just so the sheep would even have all the wool on them! She had planned this all along! Pueblo would solve this problem tomorrow.

The next day Maria was up in the mountains tending the flock of sheep when Pueblo rode up on his horse. Maria thought, "Oh no not another argument! "She would not quit now with only one week left until she completed her agreement and selected her forty sheep. She would use all her knowledge of sheep to pick the forty best sheep after all the hell Pueblo was putting her through. Miguel would be as happy as Maria when they both worked together this fall and sheared their forty sheep.

For the first time after four years of hard work Maria would finally have some cash money. Maria figured that she would get twenty five cents for the wool they sheared from each of her sheep. With forty sheep she would get ten dollars of cash money when she sold the wool this fall! She felt so proud that she had stuck it out for the four years to earn her forty sheep!

She would have her own spending money; never had she worked so hard for anything in her life. Her first purchase would be the white cloth material for her wedding dress. Maria looked up at Pueblo as Pueblo yelled at her, "You are not getting any of my sheep." Then Pueblo raised up his rifle and murdered Maria! Yes Pueblo thought that solved his problem; he would blame it on raiding Apaches. He would say Apaches came and shot her down!

★★★★

Pueblo saved a lot of money over the years. On a trip to town one day he had found a boot that a drunken cowboy had lost. Pueblo took the boot home with him and used it as a bank where he stored his money. This money, Pueblo kept buried under an old log he often sat on while he watched his sheep grazing in the hills around him. Every week Pueblo would dig up his money and count it. When Pueblo died, he had no intention of leaving the money he had worked, stolen, and murdered to obtain. So Pueblo's spirit would sit on the log where he could keep a close eye on his money. He liked to count his money when he was alive, but now that he had died he could no longer dig up the boot or lift a single coin. In fact he could hold nothing!

A hundred feet away sat Maria's spirit. She watched the log, and the man who had murdered her. She also wanted her sheep or her money! It was not right that Pueblo had murdered her and cheated her out of her rightfully earned sheep or the money! Those sheep were worth a hundred and twenty dollars and she had worked four years to earn that money! Maria would not leave without her money!

★★★★

Miguel's spirit still rides his horse; on the night of the quarter moon; on the same night of the week that he raced the Comanche warriors. On that night every month, the evening starts near the arroyo the Comanche warriors rode out from on the southwest corner of the Oscura Mountains. From there, Miguel spurs his horse into a run. Across the staked plains towards Socorro, you will find the young man riding his horse trying again and again to do his very best to outride the Comanche chasing him! Should you see him crossing the White Sands Missile Range riding to the northwest say a Prayer for Miguel and all the other spirits like Miguel that GOD will send an Angel to help them return home, in love and light. When you see Miguel coming, he appears as a bouncing ball of light. But do not get too close as he may think you are another Comanche coming to hurt him! He has been hurt enough. Just say a prayer to GOD, asking him to send his Angels, to help those in need, to go home to his love.

★★★★

John, an older man in his fifties, talked Dancing Wind into looking for Pueblo's boot of gold and silver dollars. Dancing Wind had her tracking teacher Dan, come along for the trip. The trip they took got them into the area that Pueblo lived an hour before sunset. Then they made camp setting up their tents and putting their sleeping bags inside. As the sun set they were eating a stew they fixed as they sat on the tailgate of the pickup truck.

When morning came, prayers were said, that the spirits would be willing to go *home* in the evening. Should the spirits come to camp, they would do their best to help them go *home*. Then the two older men, John and Dan, along with Dancing Wind started walking to the northeast towards a wooded canyon in the distance.

At the first barbed wire fence, Dancing Wind and Dan took off their backpacks and handed them across the fence. John kept his backpack on and climbed over the top of the fence. When he was standing on the top of the barbed wire, he lost his balance and crashed down on top of Dancing Wind, knocking Dancing Wind and her pack she had just put back on, face first into the dirt. Then the canister of bear repellent in the back of Dancing Wind's back pack discharged into John's face! The bear repellant is like a very strong tear gas. In moments, the tear gas filled the air! Suddenly John could no longer see.

Dancing Wind got the worst of the tear gas as it settled upon her. Almost immediately all of her skin was on fire. The burning tear gas was especially bad on her face, under her arms and between her legs. The tear gas strongly attacks the moist parts of one's skin! Dancing Winds eyes were burning and she could not even see. Fortunately help was at hand!

Fifty feet past the barbwire fence was a windmill and stock tank. So Dan kindly led Dancing Wind over to the stock tank and told her to hold her breath. When Dancing Wind asked why? There was no reply but she felt herself lifted by her belt and the back of her collar and flying through the air! Moments later there was a splash as Dancing Wind, clothes and all went under the water of the stock tank. Her head burst out of the water with her screaming from the temperature of the icy cold water!

Then Dan led John who also could not see over to the stock tank and repeated the process throwing him into the water too! After about ten minutes of washing the tear gas off them, they both climbed out of the stock tank. Pools of water and mud formed on the ground where the two wet prospectors stood.

Dan asked them if they wanted to call it a day or press on. They both wanted to continue, but it was clear John was mad about the tear gas and being thrown into the stock tank. Shortly thereafter, they crossed another barbed wire fence. Dancing Wind led them both into the pasture area where Pueblo used to graze his sheep.

The pasture area was surrounded by twenty and thirty foot piñon trees. Where the stream once ran was now dry. On the north slope of the pasture was an old log and here John, Dancing Wind, and Dan set their packs down and began their search. Dan sat down on the log and grudgingly Pueblo's spirit had to scoot over. They both watched as Dancing Wind and John set up plastic pegs and string to begin their grid search!

Pueblo watched as they set up the metal detector and began their search. At first he was curious what they were doing. Slowly realization dawned on Pueblo that they were looking for his boot of money! Beside Pueblo, Dan sat on the log, too. Between Dan's feet eight inches under the ground's surface was the boot of gold and silver! Pueblo and Dan both sat on the log and watched the trackers in action.

First the pegs were pounded into the ground and then a string was run between the pegs forming a grid pattern. John got mad at Dancing Wind because she had run the grid pattern up and down the slope instead of parallel to the slope. "Dumb women." He thought.

Dancing Wind saw her mistake and thought, "I will correct the mistake the next time I lay out a grid pattern."

They searched the area in the grid and did not find anything! John was mad.

Dancing Wind wanted to explore with the metal detector just to the East of the Grid in an area of rocks when she asked John for help he got mad at her and refused to help her. He was here for the money, not helping a girl who could not even do a grid pattern properly. Obviously the money was no longer here!

Dancing Wind talked to her Lily her Guardian Angel. The Angel told Dancing Wind that they had properly tracked the trail into the canyon. When Dancing Wind asked Lily, "Where should I look? "

Lily would not tell her where. The Angel simply told her: *"Go look! "*

So Dancing Wind searched with John to the east of the grid. As John thought it might be there to the east. Then John sat down and sulked. He would search no more! Dancing Wind broadened the search area going more to the west then to the north. She found nothing.

Dan asked Dancing Wind, "Why are you not working with John anymore? "

Dancing Wind said, "John is mad at me. I will search any place John wants to search with the metal detectors, but when I want to pick an area to search, John just gets angry and refuses to help me."

Then Dancing Wind searched to the north of where Dan sat. Dan sat on the log just smoking his pipe.

The sheep herder, Pablo (ghost) kept turning to Dan and asking: *"Are they going to find it? "*

Dan replied to the Sheep herder: *"Well let's wait and just see."*

Before the day was out, John and Dancing Wind had effectively searched to north, east, south and west of Dan. Dan just sat on the rock and smoked his pipe. Occasionally he would walk over and talk with Dancing Wind and try and get her to work with John. Occasionally, Dan walked over and talked with John trying to get him to work with Dancing Wind. Always Dan returned to his log and continued smoking his pipe.

John was mad at Dan too; obviously Dan was of no help, all he did was sit on a log and smoke his pipe; he obviously was incapable of finding a treasure.

After a four hour search for Pueblo's boot, Dancing Wind and John gave up. Dan, Dancing Wind, and John packed up their backpacks and returned to the car. John drove off in his pickup in a cloud of dust as he floored his engine, spinning his rear wheels as he drove off mad. Dan and Dancing Wind got into Dancing Winds jeep and headed for town. Dancing Wind announced the first thing she wanted to do was get out of her clothes, take a two hour shower then get into clean clothes.

As Dan and Dancing Wind drove towards Albuquerque, Dancing Wind asked her tracking teacher what went wrong. She told Dan, "I asked my Guardian Angel, and Lily told me that I had properly tracked the trail to the correct canyon."

She also told Dan that if Pueblo and Maria were there at the camp then the money was in the camp. For she was sure that both at the Stollsteimer River and there at the sheepherder camp, the reason the spirits were in the camp was that the gold or money was holding the spirits there.

Dan turned to Dancing Wind as she drove the jeep towards Albuquerque and replied, "You are correct, the money is holding the spirits in those locations. But when there is greed, anger, impatience, disrespect, or indifference involved that one cannot track a trail in the spirit! It just does not work! You properly tracked the trail into the correct canyon. Now each of you walked by the treasure at least twelve times. Between the two of you, there was a good search to the north, east, south and west of the treasure. But there was no cooperation between the two of you! You could see and feel the anger and impatience! Neither was there honor and respect in either your thoughts or your actions! That is why you recovered NO treasure! Literally you both got impatient and angry with each other. Had love, compassion, and cooperation been flowing between everyone, your Angels would have gone all out to help you both!

In actual, fact you both did an effective search; all 360 degrees around the boot full of treasure! The treasure was between my feet, beneath the log I sat on while I smoked my pipe! All you would have had to do was cooperate and work together in a loving manner and do your best and the Angels would have worked hard to help you! You both would have had the treasure you searched for; and in the evening both of the spirits would have wanted your help returning *home*! If there had been real cooperation, and you both went into the search in love and intending the highest good for all, the desired result would have been achieved! Certainly that is what the five Angels in the clearing watching you desired, the greatest or highest good for everyone! "

You can PROSPECT / TRACK / WORK on mountains high
You can PROSPECT / TRACK / WORK on deserts low
But the best place for you to PROSPECT / TRACK / WORK
IS WHERE YOUR ANGELS ADVISE YOU TO GO!

72 Hours in the Sonoran Desert

John McGregor thought that his life had passed him by. He met a woman, they were married, raised their children, who were grown and on their own and had been divorced for nineteen years. At sixty-nine and living on Social Security he had only two hobbies: chatting on his C. B. radio and flying his Cherokee 140 airplane out of the dirt runway beside his house out in the desert.

He lived in a small brown adobe thirty miles out of Tucson with no electricity except for a 12 volt solar panel on his roof to charge his batteries which powered his C. B. radio, and lights. He did not mind being off the power grid as it kept his bills down. His drinking water came off his metal roof where he captured the scattered rain fall which occurred in sudden short desert down pours.

John McGregor's Federal Aviation Administration (F. A. A.) pilot's license as well as his certification to legally fly his aircraft had expired four years ago but the F. A. A. would never find him out in the desert. Without his airworthy certification he could not land at the legal airports, but he could not afford either the rent of the tie downs nor the F. A. A. certified mechanic who would charge him $55 to change the oil on his engine. On his occasional trips to town he purchased his oil and an oil filter at Wal-Mart and he would illegally change the oil on his Cherokee 140 himself.

He felt old, unwanted, and over the hill except when he was flying his old aircraft. He only felt alive now days when he was flying her across the desert exploring new country. He knew the water holes for two hundred miles in every direction as he easily spotted the waterholes from the air. He just looked for the patches of green vegetation among the shades of gray, black, and brown as he flew over the desert below him. It was important to know where water was in the desert in case his old engine gave out and he had to put his aircraft down in the desert and walk.

It all started one night when a friend of a friend from a tour of service in Vietnam raised him on his CB radio and asked him to meet two teenage girls for dinner. Since they were also buying, he drove to Tucson to see what they wanted and to discuss and enjoy the steak dinner they would pay for before he told them "NO! "

John thought he would listen to the two teenagers' idea of how to make easy money flying in a load of drugs from Mexico, and then he would tell the girls to take a hike. He would not deal in drugs.

Four days later

John McGregor was sitting on the bed in this motel room he had rented for the two girls. John had not felt so alive in years. GOD it felt good! As he sat there he thought about his time in Vietnam and compared it to the events which had occurred during the last 72 hours! Some say war is hell, but Sergeant John McGregor had never felt so alive in his life as he lay in wait for the Viet Cong in a night ambush he had set into motion. On a rainy night he would take his patrol out and lie in wait, hiding behind the dike of a field of rice paddies. Beside him were six men he trusted with his life. By working as a team, they had each saved the lives of all the members of the patrol. Tonight, as they lay in the mud and were soaked by the scattered rain showers, he was scanning the area through his starlight night scope. If the Viet Cong came, he would spring his ambush. Most Americans soldiers would stay in the safety of their base on a night like this, which made it a perfect time for the Viet Cong to travel and move supplies. The VC would not expect any Americans to be out on a night like tonight. That was the reason Sergeant John McGregor was here now, looking through his night scope scanning the green and white images seeking out the enemy. All of his senses were alert to the slightest change in the sounds of the night which would signal the approach of the Viet Cong into his trap.

He missed the good old days; he missed Vietnam, his men, and the action. He did not give a damn about the five one hundred dollar bills in his wallet. If he wasted one of them buying the girls a nice leisurely dinner, he would do it in an instant. He wanted to know the rest of the story. It is not every day he gets to rescue two girls running for their lives across the Sonoran Desert, nor every day that he had live fire directed at him; and he damn well knew the flashes of gun fire when they are aimed at him! Whoever the girls had been running from were trying their best to kill him by shooting his aircraft down.

Molly, the red headed girl, was lying face down on the bed snoring. Her eyes had opened momentarily as he unlaced her dusty old boots and pulled them off her feet after she collapsed on the bed. She was sleeping in her dusty clothes with a 9mm Glock in her right hand. In the bathroom he could hear Dancing Wind, a teenage Indian girl, singing. He knew her 9mm Glock was in the shower with her. There was a chair propped under the motel room door knob and both locks were locked. Beside him on the bed were the 9mm Beretta carbine, and the extra magazine of ammo that he had agreed to deliver to the teenagers in Mexico.

When Dancing Wind got out of the shower and dressed, he expected her to wake Molly for her shower. After the girls showered and cleaned up, he could take them out for dinner. He would just have to try and wait for the story; he wanted to know the story!

As John waited uncomfortably on the second bed, he looked at the three gold bars. Never had he seen or handled old Spanish gold bars with the royal seal of King Charles of Spain. These gold bars were unlike anything he ever imagined. The bars of gold were about twelve inches long and one inch high and one inch wide.

What he wanted to know was how two teenage girls could track a three hundred year old trail, and recover three gold bars in 72 hours! He also wanted to know about the men trying to kill the girls!

Four days earlier

John had gone to the steak dinner the two teenagers had invited him to. He had expected them to make the same offer he had been made many times before--to use his Cherokee aircraft to smuggle drugs out of Mexico. He always told the smugglers "NO! "Over dinner, the girls told him they had been hired to track a trail down in the Sonoran Desert of Mexico. Whoever heard of kids now days who could track? These girls felt they could track a trail that was made three hundred years ago! He knew that was impossible, yet what they requested of him was reasonable; so he was unable to say no to the teenage girls.

Dancing Wind and Molly O'Brien told him that they felt that they would be double-crossed by the men who had hired them to track the trail. He listened to their story, and when they had told him this farfetched story about them being trackers he decided to catch the two girls in a lie. John simply asked them to show him the contract where they were hired to track a trail. He had let them spin there lies long enough and just wanted to see the expression on their faces when he trapped them in the lies they were feeding him. John was not born yesterday. So he told the teenagers: "Show me the contract."

Molly pulled the contract from her pocket.

His jaw dropped to the table, and he picked it up and read it. Who in their right mind would pay two girls $500 a day to track a trail? Uncle Sam only paid him about $319 a month when he fought in Vietnam! Here were the signatures and the addresses of the men who had hired them on the contract in black and white though.

So he asked the girls what they wanted. They wanted two duffel bags air dropped into Old Mexico. One duffel bag was to be dropped off prior to the girls going into Mexico, and one if they called for help. The first black ballistic nylon bag contained six half gallon canteens of water, two M. R. E. 's (meals ready to eat), a first aid kit, and a Glock 9mm semi-automatic with three ten round magazines, and a flare gun with signal flares in the Olin orange container. The second black bag was identical to the first except it also contained a 9mm Beretta carbine, three loaded magazines for the rifle but without the Olin flare package. He only had to deliver the second bag if they called for help on their CB radios.

He told them: "Never will I land my aircraft in Mexico to help you ladies. The risk is just too high for me. What I will do for you though is cross the border for up to twenty minutes. Ten minutes will put us twenty miles south of the American border at 120 miles per hour. Another ten minutes flight time will get me back into the United States."

John said he would call it a momentary navigational error; should he ever be questioned about his "accidentally" crossing the United States border into Mexico. At 6: 00 the next morning, as the sun was just beginning to rise in the east, the two girls accompanied him across the border at 250 feet above the ground as the aircraft dropped the first package off. By keeping the aircraft low he intended to prevent the detection of his aircraft on radar by the Mexican or American authorities.

Molly fixed the position of the drop on her Garmin G. P. S. and told Dancing Wind when to drop the package. In the ninety seconds before the drop was made John pulled back the throttle of his engine slowing it as much as possible. John wanted to minimize any damage to the package that he was planning to air drop by slowing the aircraft as slow as possible and so it did not get damaged in the drop.

He was getting the Cherokee aircraft down really close to the ground. He also adjusted the flaps to the third position for landing the aircraft as he wanted maximum lift to keep the aircraft aloft. He would not land. But he brought the plane down to within fifteen feet of the ground as he slowed the aircraft to 90 miles per hour. Then as Molly watched the GPS for the proper coordinates, she told Dancing Wind when to release the package.

John immediately began applying power to the engine as he decreased the flap settings and the airspeed increased. Ten and a half minutes later the Cherokee crossed back into US airspace and then they all relaxed and breathed easier. They had successfully prepositioned their critical supplies twenty miles south of the American border in the hot dry; Sonoran Desert of Mexico.

★★★★

John dropped the teenagers at the bus station in Tucson and saw them get on the 9: 30 Greyhound bus to Nogales. There in Nogales, the girls told him, they would be picked up by Johnny Torres and Poncho Hernandez who had hired them to track the trail into Mexico. Molly and Dancing Wind knew that the trail that they would be tracking was a trail to a Jesuit silver mining site on a small mountain about twenty nine miles south of the U. S. border.

At 11: 30, the Greyhound bus pulled into the border crossing at Nogales. When crossing the border into Mexico, the two teenagers had their backpacks searched by the Mexican Crossing Guards. Watching them being searched were the two men they had come to Mexico to track for: Johnny Torres and Poncho Hernandez, both men gave a knowing glance to the other.

The two teenagers were unarmed, or the Mexican border guards would have found their weapons and arrested them both. Both men gave them welcoming smiles and held out their hands to shake with the two trackers that they had hired. Molly O'Brien looked at the two smiling men and they reminded her of two wolves welcoming two sheep to join them for dinner. Both men were dressed entirely in black. Black hats, black shirts, black jeans and black boots; but what disturbed Molly the most was the black auras, the light around their bodies. Molly glanced at Dancing Wind and gave her a look which said, "What did you get me into? "

They all piled into the truck and Johnny Torres drove them to a grocery store where Dancing Wind had asked them to stop so she could do some last minute shopping.

There Dancing Wind went in and purchased two loaves of bread, a half dozen packages of assorted lunch meat, and a block of cheese and eighteen bottles of water. She put the food in the large ice cooler that Johnny had in the back of his truck. While Johnny had offered to help the girls squeeze in up front with them the teenagers declined and said that they would be more comfortable riding back in the bed of the pickup truck.

Johnny and Poncho got into the front cab while Dancing Wind, Molly O'Brien and four Angels jumped into the back of the truck with the two teenagers. Johnny and Poncho looked at each other and smiled; this was easier than anything that they ever imagined. As they drove west out of Nogales, Poncho recovered his .44 caliber revolver and his two throwing knives that he had placed under the seat before they entered the border crossing station to pick up the two stupid gringos. Poncho also handed Johnny his holster and .357 magnum revolver that he had also hidden beneath the seat. Johnny stuck the gun under his shirt which was worn loosely over his pants. The belt kept his pants from falling down as Johnny had an extra forty pounds he carried on his beer belly. For four hours they drove west and a little south. Their speed had fallen considerably as the dirt roads got progressively worse.

Normally, it was hot in the summer, but this week had been hotter than usual, it was a real scorcher. It was 108 degrees F. in the shade and there was very little shade out in the Sonoran Desert. At night it cooled down to ninety degrees. The sun seemed to draw the moisture out of everything. The only plants which seemed to survive out here had sharp needles or thorns on every leaf or branch.

★★★★

Juan was lost in thought, how was he going to get his mother a window made out of real glass for the living room of the small adobe where he, his mother, and sister lived? In the winter, his mom wove rugs from wool they obtained from the small herd of goats they owned. The goat provided his family with food and wool.

He sure would like glass to put in the window so the wind in the winter did not blow into the living room and bother his mother's fingers as she used her loom. Juan had four or five months to figure out where he could get a real glass window for his mom. It was hard being the man of the house when you are only thirteen years old.

★★★★

Juan saw them coming a long way off. He recognized the black truck and immediately started herding his goats away from the mountain as he knew that the mean men were again returning to his hill. He wanted to be gone before they arrived.

The first time the men had driven up on him, the men saw one of his goats in the road,instead of slowing their truck to avoid hitting his goat, they had accelerated and deliberately killed his goat. Then, they had laughed about his goat dying. He needed the goats to make the cheese his mother and he made and sold. Juan herded his goats away from the mountain as fast as he could; he needed to be gone from this place now that the mean men were returning.

The truck arrived at the base of the three hundred foot mountain and everyone got out of the truck and stretched their legs. The men were anxious to get started they had agreed to pay the two trackers a thousand dollars or four days pay to get them to come track at their site. One thousand dollars was paid in advance, and they had promised the trackers another thousand dollars and an equal share of recovery of the treasure that they searched for.

Since they had searched for three years and failed to find any treasure, they decided that they needed expert help, which is why they had finally decided to hire the trackers who specialized in tracking the Old Spanish Trails. The trackers they hired were supposed to be good. They better be good for the two thousand dollars that they had agreed to pay them for four days work.

When the two women tracked the trail to the cache site where there treasure was buried the agreement was to pay the trackers another thousand dollars. Johnny and Pancho did not have the second half of the money they had promised to pay the women but they knew the women were dependent on them, as it was thirty five miles to the closest town and they held the keys to the only way out in their pockets.

To the north there was nothing but the hot dry Sonoran Desert for twenty-nine miles where you reached a fence marking the United States border. But once you reached the border it was still desert for another ten miles until you reached Arivaca, the closest town north of the border to them. There was no way two teenage girls could possibly cross thirty-nine miles of desert in this summer heat. If the girls failed to find Arivaca they could easily have fifty miles of desert to cross with no water anywhere. No one would travel north across the desert. The other ways out of their camp were even more remote. Both men knew those girls were not going anywhere.

Johnny and Poncho wanted the women to begin tracking immediately but both Dancing Wind and Molly politely refused saying that they had not eaten all day. As they would be tracking for hours, they told the men they would do better work on a full stomach, rather than only thinking about returning to the truck to eat.

Both men reluctantly agreed to eat first. They went into one cooler and got themselves some tacos and some Corona beers. Molly and Dancing Wind then began making themselves sandwiches as they drank the bottled water. Dancing Wind, after eating, made four extra large sandwiches piling on an inch of meats and another inch with thick chunks of cheese between the slices of bread, these she wrapped up and stuck in her back pack along with two bottles of water.

Poncho and Johnny looked at each other as they saw Dancing Wind wander off to the west, lost in thought as she absently walked away from camp. Both men thought to themselves "These girls are supposed to be trackers? "

Molly then distracted both men by asking them to show her the Spanish markers that they had located on the small mountain. When they asked Molly where Dancing Wind was going she replied that Dancing Wind was going to interrogate the goat herder they had seen moving his goats off the mountain to the west. Molly told the men that the goat herder would never realize Dancing Winds intentions as she was very skillful in asking questions about any Spanish markers and triangles he may have seen. Satisfied with what Molly said, the two men began showing Molly the Spanish markers scattered across their treasure mountain.

The boy herding his family's goats westward could not move his herd as fast as Dancing Wind walked towards him. He wanted to get away from those bad people but he simply could not leave his goats.

The goats were the only way he had of putting food on the table for his mother and sister. Then he slowly realized it was only a girl walking towards him. The men were not coming also, so he relaxed just a little after finding two big fist size stones he could throw at the girl if she tried to hurt him. He watched the skinny Indian girl approach him. She certainly did not look dangerous. She motioned him to sit with her in the shade of a large boulder and slowly he sat down beside her. Dancing Wind told the boy her name and asked Juan his name. Soon they were talking and the boy realized that the woman was crazy.

She pulled four of the thickest sandwiches the boy had ever seen out of her back pack. Juan eyed the sandwiches, and they looked over two inches thick with many slices of meat and cheese, never had he seen such thick sandwiches. Then she told him she will trade the four sandwiches to Juan if he will promise to do five things for her.

Juan would have agreed to anything to get his hands on one of those thick sandwiches. Juan had not eaten anything but a small bowl of beans in two days. Food had been awfully hard to come by since his father had left to cross the desert to the north eight years ago and never returned.

The first thing Dancing Wind asked Juan for that he take his goats and go elsewhere for a week as she told Juan the men with her were not very nice men. Juan immediately agreed as he was already trying to leave the area as fast as he could.

The second thing she asked for, as she pulled out ten feet of half inch rope out of her bag, was that he learned to tie a knot called a bowline knot. Then she tied the knot in both ends of the rope and had him tie the knot with her many times over twenty minutes as she told him how it can be tied around a tree to hold a heavy load.

Then Dancing Wind made her third request and she handed over another sandwich. She pulled out some quarter inch nylon rope from her pack and showed Juan how to tie a second knot, called a pursik, that could easily slide up the thicker rope but when weight is applied it locks into the thicker rope. Then Dancing Wind told Juan how, together, these two knots could be used to climb up a cliff. The bowline would secure the rope at the top of the cliff and the prusik knot allowed a climber to easily go up the secured rope. Dancing Wind took her time talking about the knots as she had the boy repeatedly tie and retie the knots.

Her fourth request was that Juan always obeys his mother.

Her fifth request was that Juan say his prayers at night to GOD. Juan promised to learn his knots, obey his mom and say his prayers. Dancing Wind then handed over the remaining two sandwiches. After spending an hour with Juan, Dancing Wind got up to leave. As she walked away,she reminded the boy he must leave the area for a week. She stopped and turned taking one last look at Juan and said, "Don't forget to pray and GOD will answer your prayers." Then she was gone.

Juan would tell his mother and sister about the crazy woman he met today. As he ate one of the thick sandwich he knew that he would take the other three sandwiches home with him now. Tonight he would surprise his sister and his mom with the sandwiches and they would all eat like kings!

Those were interesting knots the girl showed him. He never knew that girls knew about knots. He would practice the knots as he walked home herding his goats in front of him. Next to the boy, his Guardian Angel walked along with his charge, the Angel smiled, as he was proud of the boy for saving food for his sister and mother. The Angel was also very happy that his prayer was answered that someone would come and help the family since his father had gone *home* to GOD. Yes, even Angels pray to GOD.

When Dancing Wind returned to the small mountain, she walked with Molly, Johnny and Poncho as they showed her the Spanish markers on the mountain. When the men asked Dancing Wind about what she had learned about any Spanish Markers the boy may have seen, Dancing Wind replied he doesn't know anything except about herding goats and making cheese from the goats' milk. Dancing Wind did not tell the men what she really did with the boy; it was none of their business, she was just following her Guardian Angel, Lily's instructions to teach the boy two knots that mountain climbers frequently use. The sandwiches simply had been Dancing Winds idea.

As they walked across the mountain, the two teenagers were carefully looking at the numerous rock formations as they listen to both men's explanations of where they had searched. Occasionally, an Angel pointed out a Spanish marker to the teenagers. The two trackers view of the mountain was quiet different from what most people saw when they looked at the same mountain. What they saw was a circular clearing surrounded by big high boulders. Johnny described the difficult time he had breathing the day he had explored the clearing looking for treasure. The girls knew to keep clear of the circle as they saw the spirits that stood guard over the treasures inside the circle and recognized it would not be an easy recovery and walked on.

They saw an immense snake coming out of the ground whose head was over a hundred feet across. Because the snake in the Bible represents the Devil tempting Adam and Eve, they knew they would be tempted by what was there on the mountain. The snake also told them that there would be many death traps.

They saw Indian and Spanish hieroglyphs, so they took the time to read what they said. In the hieroglyphs, the teenagers read about how to use three triangles of stone to locate the entrance to the tunnel the snakes guarded. The hieroglyphs also showed their position relative to the triangles so they knew that one triangle stone would be north of them and another triangle stone would be east of them. Possibly the stone they were reading from now was the third triangle position. They also saw the dead upside down Indians in various parts of the descriptive pictures; that was not good as it implied that there were many death traps associated with the cache. The moon in the hieroglyphs told them that the cache was mostly bars of silver bullion. The counter clockwise spiral told them that they would have to descend into a hole or shaft to locate the treasure. Unfortunately, they felt the treasure would require considerable effort and probably an earth digging excavator to safely make a recovery, so they walked on.

They saw a twenty-five foot high boulder with the two arrows at its base pointing where to dig, and the broken heart chiseled into the stone above the arrows. The face of one stoneman looked out keeping watch, while a second stone face looked down at the ground where the stone door would be located about seven feet under the surface of the ground.

****Spanish Death Trap- One face is looking out to the left and the second face is looking down to where the stone door is located. When the door is opened the trap is activated. ***

Six feet to the right of the two arrows was a flat stone, standing upright, which reminded the women of a tombstone or a grave. Molly figured the kill zone this death trap encompassed was not less than two thousand square feet. It would be more deadly than a modern claymore mine currently used by the U. S. Army. Briefly a grin came across Molly's face as she realized the humor the builders of this site had shown her. Then the grin disappeared before anyone but Dancing Wind had seen Molly's expression. So the trackers walked on, leaving the death trap alone and they continued to track the old trails. Johnny and Poncho never saw the Spanish Markers and the many stone doors that they walked by.

The trackers stopped for two minutes to look at the fifteen foot long snake whose body was parallel to the ground except the head which turned down towards the ground. A five foot tall fox was standing on his two back legs pointing to the snake and to the boulder beside where the snake's head was looking. The snake and the fox were shadow markers cut into the stone. There would be a stone door down where the snake looked; all Johnny and Poncho saw was a fifteen foot high wall of stone. They failed to see that the rock wall had been chipped out so that at noon the shadows cast by the sun showed the snake and the fox.

As the two teenagers tracked the trails they were beginning to understand the early miners and priest and the way they thought. They wanted a very good understanding of how the early death traps worked and the symbols used to mark them. For when a door was actually entered, their understanding of the traps, how the attack would occur and the symbols used to mark the death trap, would determine if they left the site alive.

One particular interesting site held them spell bound for five minutes. It consisted of an opening in the boulders that looked like a doorway where after walking in the door, one was expected to dig a hole into the ground in order to go any further. They felt sure that there was a stone door buried about five to seven feet deep. When the door was opened, sand would pour out and the boulders would collapse upon anyone who had foolishly opened the door.

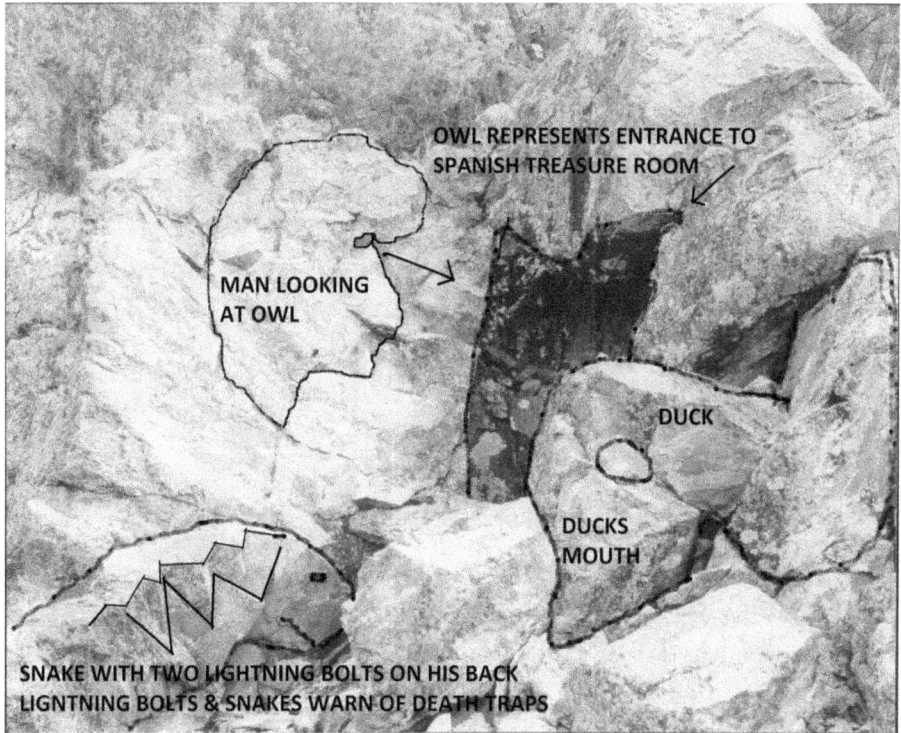

Notice the black shadow of the owl in this Spanish death trap

Looking into the entrance way, they saw a stone horse and a snake traveling up to the doorway. The large stone snake was on the left side of the entrance way. On the back of the snake was the jagged design of a lightning bolt. The door itself was shaped like an owl, with the shapes of owls carved into either side of it. The owl is used by the Spanish to represent a treasure room where the bars of gold and silver are stored. The entire site consisted of six huge boulders. Three boulders represented the left wall, the roof or ceiling and the right side. The forth boulder formed the back wall. Two boulders were on the left of the door, kind of leading up to or guiding one to the stone entrance. Both teenagers admired the ingenuity and craftsmanship of the builders, but it was just too easy; they felt the Spanish would never make it so easy for anyone to locate their treasure storage rooms.

After admiring the site, the two girls listened to Lily, Dancing Winds Guardian Angel explain that the doorway was underground. As one dug a hole, the stability of the two boulders standing on the left and the one used as the right wall would be undermined possibly leading to the boulder on the roof and the right wall coming down abruptly on top of the diggers. Lily explained to the teenagers that it was another death trap. The builders intended that when people saw the owls they were supposed to be overcome by greed and fail to see the death trap warning signs: the horse, the snake and the lightning bolt on top of the snake and be lured into the death trap.

Poncho and Johnny thought that this must be the spot for them to dig as the women were standing so long looking at this site. Just as they were about to ask if this is where they were to dig both women turned without saying a word and walked on. As the trackers traveled on toward the small mountain, it was not one site they saw but an accumulation of mines, treasures, caches and death traps placed here over the centuries. To dig them all would take months to possibly years of work. The trackers would look over the hill and pick one best site, and this doorway they just left while very interesting was not a door that either woman would willingly choose to try and enter.

In a dry arroyo, the two women stopped for a few minutes to pray and ask the Nature Spirits for permission to prospect on the mountain. They planted some dry land beans here as an offering to Mother Nature.

Stone bird

** Picture of Stone Heart**

Fifteen minutes later, the teenagers walked by a five foot high stone heart measuring fifteen feet across. The Spanish used the heart to symbolize gold, the men never saw the heart, and the teenagers never mentioned the treasure symbol to them. Underneath the heart there would be a stone door. But in the trackers experience, eleven out of twelve times previously, a stone door under a heart was trapped. They had no heavy equipment that could move a fifteen ton stone heart, so they walked on continuing to explore the mountain.

Before the evening came, the trackers had seen one map chiseled into a flat stone, and they saw stone bears, which they knew could spring to life in an instant and jump five to

ten feet. These stone bears they wanted to stay away from. There were foxes, numerous stone snakes, a throne, a crown, the mountain lion, a stone man and woman, there were three stone men climbing the hill with packs on their backs that the girls also saw.

★★ When Dancing Wind looked through the stone mans eye, she saw the next Jesuit Priest stone marker that she needed to travel to locate the hidden stone door★★

The two men walking beside them simply failed to see what was in front of their eyes. The stone hearts,stone horses, and horse heads, the marker for the location of the centuries old digging tools, the birds in flight and the birds and eagles sitting on the ground or giving directions, wolves,and Indians were just some of the many Jesuit markers they walked past. They saw the markers for the locations of the stone maps or "P" stones. They viewed over thirty five Spanish death traps; yes this certainly was an interesting site.

** Picture of a stone bird **

60 foot long stone Eagle or Shelter Bird

Before leaving the mountain, Molly O'Brien repeated the

agreement verbally to both men to refresh their memory as to what they had agreed to. They were here to do the tracking. The men had to dig the holes and they would probably dig four of five holes before Molly and Dancing Wind would be able to get them inside the treasure room.

When Dancing Wind got the men to a stone door that they could go inside, then they were to get the second thousand dollars and each of them would get an equal share of the recovery. The trackers would not be going underground or into the treasure room. The men agreed again to the terms that they had agreed to a week earlier in the written agreement. Then Molly again told them, "It may take us one to five tries to get you into the proper stone door so they could enter the treasure room, as each site was different."

Then Molly pointed to a wedge shaped stone up on a pedestal of another flat stone. The wedge pointed to a flat rock wall fifteen feet high. In direct alignment with the stone wedge was a four foot high wedge in white caliches could clearly be seen on the black rock pointing straight down into the ground. As the sun was setting Molly said "We will start here at first light."

Reluctantly the two men agreed it would be best to start in the morning and all four of them left the mountain where the Jesuits mined silver three hundred years earlier.

At six in the morning they all ate a large breakfast of bacon, eggs and pancakes. The men had hot coffee to get them started in the morning. Both teenagers had one of the bottles of water.

After drinking the water they went out and walked away from the camp to use the bathroom. When they returned they each checked their packs and ensured that the two half gallon canteens they each carried were full of water. They were going to walk up the hill to where the men were already digging but the two Angels there in camp pointed to the cooler, as they wanted the trackers to drink another bottle of water.

Molly told the Angels: "What do you think we are, camels? "

Both Angels smiled and said, *"Drink the water."*

When the girls each finished the second bottle of cold water, they slipped on their back packs. As they started to walk up the hill, standing in front of them were the two Angels, pointing to the ice cooler with the water.

Dancing Wind said: "Not again Lily, I cannot hold any more water." With a full water bottle in hand the girls walked up the hill.

Three and a half hours later, Poncho and Johnny hit the stone door. Dancing Wind insisted they expand the hole just a little on all four sides so she could read any symbols that were engraved in stone. There were two symbols. A blood red stone heart was placed squarely in the middle of the square stone door. To the left of the door was a lightning bolt pointed directly at the stone door.

Johnny told the girls to get down in the hole with them and help them pry the door open. Poncho, the more dangerous of the two, sensed something was wrong. The trackers showed no excitement, nor did they jump into the hole when clearly they had tracked the three hundred year old trail to a stone door.

Dancing Wind told the men that they were going to open the door her way. On three sides of the stone door were hand holds but in one corner was a place to fasten a rope. She had the men get some come-a-longs and rope and then tie the rope to the door.

With one rope attached to the stone door and another rope around some large stone boulders twenty feet away which would not move, Dancing Wind had the men pull the door open with some come-a-longs placed between the ropes.

Slowly the line grew tighter and tighter until it was stretched so tight one could walk on the rope. The stone door set into place three hundred years ago started to open. Suddenly the door popped open. Out of the door poured sand filling the hole they had dug.

Dancing Wind grabbed Poncho by the arm as she yelled run and pulled him along beside her. Molly had grabbed Johnny and also yelled run at the same time her friend did.

★★ Spanish Death Trap-TRIGGER on a fast moving surface slider— the actual trap entrance-a stone door, is usually 100-200 yards down hill. When the door is opened a sand channel to this trap will release the trigger stone and this fast moving surface slider and about ten tons of boulders piled behind it will go racing down the hill to kill anyone who opens the stone door. ★★

As the girls ran for their lives, dragging the men with them, a five ton flat slider rock two hundred feet up the slope suddenly roared to life and rushed down the slope! Accompanying the five ton slider rock was another five tons of one hundred to five hundred pound boulders which came crashing down the slope! Ten tons of rocks were now piled up on top of the stone door where the four of them had been standing thirty seconds earlier.

Johnny and Poncho knew that if it had not been for the women's warning they would both be dead and buried at the bottom of the hole they just dug under ten tons of rock. Dancing Wind then asked the men if they wanted to quit or would they like the trackers to select a second door for them to dig. Both men wanted to keep trying.

Molly said: "Then all right, we will pick our second door site, but first let's take a break for lunch."

After a quick lunch the four of them climbed up the small hill again. It was 11 am. This time Dancing Wind picked the site of the stone door. Both men started to dig again. They were tired from the first hole that they had dug but the digging went quicker as they had a lot more enthusiasm as the women were better at tracking than either imagined was possible. On their first try they had actually hit a man made stone door; thirty five miles from the closest town in the middle of nowhere. Poncho and Johnny had failed to find anything in the numerous holes they had dug for the last three years.

The heat of the day was now upon them. It was 108 degrees as the hot sun beat down upon them. But they would not quit or slow down as each man thought that today he would be in the treasure room and become a millionaire.

Neither man wanted the girls to find out that they did not have the second thousand dollars they had promised to pay them. They would have never found the last door and they knew they would not have ever selected this site, as it just looked so normal. There was simply nothing here at this spot that would have encouraged them to dig here. They needed the trackers and they would not let them leave.

As the sweat poured down the men as they dug in the heat Molly asked the men if she could get them a beer. Both men said yes, so Molly and Dancing Wind went down and got them a couple of beers. Both women then took a salt tablet and a bottle of cold water. They were both drinking as much water as they could possibly hold.

At two thirty in the afternoon, both men knew they had found their second stone door. At three o'clock, the second stone door was breached! With the equipment the men had brought, they built a wooden tripod to allow them to lower one man at a time into the mine shaft they found under the door. Using half inch nylon rope and a body harness and pulleys with a four to one ratio, the trackers were able to lower the men into the hole.

Ten minutes later the men were in the treasure room. They estimated at least four tons of bullion was stacked in bars in the middle of the room waiting for them. Johnny and Poncho looked at each other and said: "We're Rich! ! ! "

Johnny and Poncho decided it was time to give Dancing Wind and Molly O'Brien their fair share. The two Angels beside Johnny and Poncho walked out of the treasure room, they would have no part in the treachery planned for the teenagers who had helped them.

Poncho liked this part almost as much as being rich. Poncho enjoyed seeing the look of terror on a woman's face as he took his knife and killed her! He liked to do his killing slow so he could enjoy it as long as possible. Both men called up to the girls to come join them and see all the treasure they had found.

Molly replied, "We never go underground, you know that, but start passing up the bullion and we will help haul it up."

Both men agreed as they might as well utilize both trackers to help haul their treasure out of the ancient tunnel where it was stored. So for thirty minutes the men loaded up buckets of bullion one bar at a time, which the teenagers hauled out of the hole. As the men worked, they discussed different ideas on how to kill their partners. Finally the men worked out a plan to catch the two teenagers by surprise. The last bucket the women hauled up contained three tiny bars of bullion weighing about six pounds each. These were tiny bars compared to all the other bars which weighed about forty pounds apiece. The stack of bars was about eighteen inches high and weighed over a thousand pounds which the trackers had placed on the edge of the west side of the hole. The greater part of the treasure was still down in the tunnel; literally tons of silver bullion, yet both men had grown impatient in dealing with their partners on top of the ancient tunnel, so they left the treasure room and walked down the tunnel to where the shaft to the surface was located.

Two Angels came up out of the mine hole and walked by the teenage girls without saying a word, they walked by with their heads looking down at their feet, and their shoulders slumped over as if under a heavy load. Partway down the hill they just stopped walking and both Angels gave one last glance up the hill.

Beside the two teenagers, another two Angels watched the first two Angels go by. One of the two Angels on top of the hill Lily, then told the two trackers, *"Take three of the small metal bars and put them in your backpacks. Go now! ! Disable the vehicle and travel to the north with all possible speed."*

Molly put one metal bar in her backpack and Dancing Wind placed two of the small metal bars of bullion in her backpack and the teenagers rapidly moved down the hill towards the vehicle. They ran past a wet circle on the ground where the four Angels hugged each other and cried. As the Angels cried, their tears wet the ground in a small circle.

The trackers each pulled a knife out of their packs and they slit the side wall of each tire. Then they cut the valve stem until they could hear the air hissing out of the slit they had made. They took the remaining two water bottles out of the coolers, and spilled the ice on the ground. Then, in a very rapid walk, the two trackers took off to the north. It was four in the afternoon as the trackers began their final run north across the Sonoran Desert.

The men planned to kill the girls as soon as they were able to get out of the hole and casually walk behind them. When they walked to the shaft tunnel hole where they had come in and called for the girls to haul them up. There was no answer, only silence. Poncho hauled on the rope he had been lowered down into the hole with and did not like it at all. The rope just pulled all the way down into the hole, falling in with him! If the second rope did the same thing, fell into the hole, they would die here! Fortunately Johnny's rope was tied at the end. It took them eighteen minutes to climb out of the hole.

At the top of the shaft, there was a pile of their treasure. They noticed that three of the very smallest metal bars of gold were missing. More important was the fact that the girls were gone! Somehow they must have heard them talking down in the shaft, they thought. That is it, their voices must have carried down the tunnel. They must get their three small bars of gold back and there must be no witnesses left alive! Never had they intend to let those girls steal their gold!

The two men ran down the hill to their truck. Damn, those girls had flattened their tires! Johnny and Poncho started running down the dirt road towards town. They would catch those girls and kill them slow! For ten minutes they ran to the east towards Nogales. When they could run no more they walked another ten minutes.

Poncho stopped and said, "Johnny, we have been tricked. There are no tracks in the road. Let's look for tracks as we walk back to the truck."

At the truck, the ice had melted into the desert sand. The men had their guns with them all day but they each grabbed an extra box of ammo and their one quart canteens of water. Johnny grabbed a beer from each of them but Poncho stopped him, and had him return the two bottles of beer to the truck bed. Poncho said "Not now, we will celebrate being rich after we have paid our partners! When there are no witnesses we will celebrate our good fortune."

The men had wasted thirty minutes at the truck and walking to the east. The trackers had a forty-eight minute head start.

Every fifteen minutes, the teenagers stopped for ninety seconds to rest and drink water. Sweat poured down their faces and the salt stung their eyes. They were not just traveling north but they were traveling north using their Gamin G. P. S. to navigate by. If they were to be alive the rest of the day, they must reach the cache where they had placed the black bag nine miles to the north.

The trackers walked fast, about four miles per hour, but they did not run. To live, they must cover the ground moving north but they could not run and risk a sprained ankle or a broken bone or any injury in a fall. Sometimes they were stopped by deep washes and had to travel east or west to find a way down and then a way up the opposite side. These detours cost them time. Even though they were not running, before long they were breathing heavy through their mouths to get enough air. The heat from the sun was intense. It seemed that the temperature had climbed to 109. Dancing Wind took a cup of water and poured it on Molly's hair to help cool her off. Then she did the same for herself. They started off again at a fast walk. Never had Molly felt so hot. She turned to her friend and asked her what she was thinking.

Dancing Wind turned to Molly and smiled; "I was thanking the sun for its life giving light, and its wonderful heat which is keeping us from being cold. I was thanking the sun for lighting our way to the north and I was especially thanking the sun for this wonderful heat! Then I was asking the wind if it would blow the hot winds across this desert."

Molly just shook her head then laughed aloud.

Johnny and Poncho were on the trail of the teenagers. They would not let them get away. Those trackers were not stealing any of their treasure! It was all theirs.

Johnny and Poncho cursed the sun, they cursed the heat, and they cursed the desert cactus too. An hour later the last of the water was gone, they threw their canteens away when they ran dry and continued following the girls' tracks north.

Two hours later the men caught sight of the two teenagers. They were closing the gap. When the two teenagers stopped to rest and drink water they saw the men behind them. They still took their full ninety seconds to drink the water, and when they had emptied out the half gallon canteen they returned it to their pack and continued north. The men were five hundred yards behind the trackers.

Thirty minutes later the two teenagers walked up to the black bag they had cached from the Cherokee 140 airplane the day before. Molly quickly removed the Glock, holster, holster belt and the spare magazines of ammo for the Glock and belted them on around her waist. Then she checked the magazine in the Glock to be sure it was fully loaded like she left it. Then she removed the safety. Before it would fire she would have to manually put one round in the chamber. Of the six canteens of water packed by them, two of the canteens had ruptured on impact when they hit the ground. Dancing Wind quickly double checked that the ruptured canteens were completely empty of water. Never would she leave any water behind. The two trackers loaded everything else in their packs and continued on. Behind them, the men had closed the distance to four hundred yards.

As they walked north, the sun beat down on the Sonoran Desert and everyone walking on it. It was hot, so very hot. As they walked north, Dancing Wind got on the CB radio she picked up from the cache and began transmitting.

"Delta Whiskey to Juliet Mike. '

"Delta Whiskey to Juliet Mike. '

" Delta Whiskey to Juliet Mike."

As they walked north towards the United States border, in front of the girls was a deep dry arroyo which climbed to a three hundred foot hill just to the north of the arroyo. Crossing the deep arroyo slowed the teenagers down a little and this was the time when Johnny and Poncho broke into a run to really put an end to their hunt. As the girls climbed out of the arroyo and started to climb the hill both men opened fired with their handguns to force the two teenagers to take shelter behind the rocks on the small hill. Once they had forced the teenagers to stop running and hide behind the rocks, they knew they would shortly surround and capture them shortly.

Dancing Wind and Molly began zig and zag as they ran up the hill. One hundred and fifty feet from the top of the hill they took shelter behind a large rock. The men looked at each other and smiled. They had them now.

As they climbed out of the arroyo both men stood beside some four to six foot tall boulders that had over the years rolled down from the top of the hill. They stopped. As one man reloaded his revolver the other man kept up a slow but steady fire at the boulders the teenagers hid behind.

One hundred and twenty yards up the hill, Molly told Dancing Wind to zig and zag as she covered her for their final run to the top and over the hill. Dancing Wind reached into Molly's back pack and took out the Olin flare package and the small bar of bullion. Dancing Wind could lighten Molly's back pack by twelve pounds. Dancing Wind and Molly briefly hugged each other and Dancing Wind prepared to run for the top of the hill as soon as Molly began firing.

Molly saw both men standing out in the open making clear targets of themselves as they slowly walked up the hill. As Poncho emptied his revolver firing at the boulder they hid behind. Then Johnny began firing his revolver at them. They both stood out in the open; one firing as the second reloaded his revolver. When they had closed the distance to one hundred yards, Molly knew now was the time to act. Molly chambered a round in her Glock. She fully intended to place three rounds in the center of body mass of her best target. She would kill both men before she let them hurt Dancing Wind. With both arms outstretched in front of her holding the Glock firmly in both hands, Molly moved eighteen inches to her right and partially stepped out from behind the shelter of the boulder so she could stop the men from continuing their attack. She quickly centered her aim on the center of Poncho's chest and began to squeeze the trigger. Just as she was about to fire, her Guardian Angel stepped in front of her gun so she jerked it to the right just as she was triggering her three 9mm bullets into the center of Poncho's body mass. All three rounds slammed into the rock immediately to the men's left splattering both men with sharp rock fragments.

Both men dropped to the ground and crawled back behind some rocks for cover. As the men lay on the ground they looked at each other and said, "How in the hell did they get the handgun thorough Mexican Customs? "

Molly O'Brien turned and sprinting up the hill and over the top immediately after the third round was fired. Dancing Wind was just over the hill on the north side talking into her CB radio.

"Delta Whiskey to Juliet Mike. '

" Delta Whiskey to Juliet Mike."

"This is Juliet Mike to Delta Whiskey. I am in bound can you give me a position."

"Juliet Mike, we will be moving north with two hostiles behind.

Give us four minutes and you will see our position."

Both women continued walking rapidly to the north. Four minutes later they stopped and seeing they had widened the distance to three hundred yards to the men behind them, they opened the Olin package and fired off a flare just as the sun was setting in the western sky. With three more flares in hand and the CB radio they continued moving to the north.

Three minutes later, they heard the sound of an aircraft. They had widened their lead by another hundred yards as they traveled north. It was the water which had made the difference allowing them to break ahead of the men pursuing them.

"Delta Whiskey where do you want the package? "

"Juliet Mike make the drop one hundred yards north of us in the direction we are traveling,I will light us up now." She lit another flare as they jogged north.

The Cherokee came by traveling south at eight hundred feet at 140 miles per hour. In the twilight of the setting sun, he saw the flashes of gunfire directed at him by the two men on the ground. He had not felt this alive in thirty years. He was happy the fools on the ground had given away their position as he would be sure to make sure his package never landed anywhere near them.

He came around and slowed his Cherokee down as much as possible and lowered his aircraft down to about thirty feet off the desert floor. Because he was operating in the fast fading light of twilight he could not descend to within fifteen feet of the ground as he had when the teenagers accompanied him to drop the first package.

As he passed over the jogging teenagers flying north, he pushed out their package right on top of them. Because he was traveling at 85 miles per hour he knew the forward momentum would carry the package fifty to one hundred yards north of the trackers.

The two teenagers headed straight for the package. Without

stopping they both reached down and each one grabbed one strap and kept on jogging north with the black duffel bag between them. When they felt that their lead on the men behind them was five hundred yards, the two teenagers stopped. Molly with her Glock in hand kept watch while Dancing Wind opened the package which had been air dropped to them. Dancing Wind picked up the Glock out of the black bag and strapped the holster on her. She checked the magazine, and it was exactly how she had left it-- fully loaded. She moved the safety to off and chambered a round then holstered her weapon. She then removed the Beretta carbine. She also checked its magazine and loaded the weapon. Then she removed the canteens of water. Three canteens had ruptured from the impact,leaving three canteens of water fully intact.

Then Dancing Wind set two of the full canteens aside and two M. R. E. 's. Then she packed both backpacks balancing out the weight between both of their backpacks. Dancing Wind then put on her backpack and in the fading twilight that occurs once the sun had set, she kept watch with the carbine in her arms while Molly put on her backpack and drank some water. Then Molly kept watch while Dancing Wind had a long drink of water.

Both men were furious that they had not been able to prevent the aircraft from dropping a package to the teenagers. For the two minutes that the aircraft was in sight, they had fired bullets from their revolvers as fast as they could aim and load them. They had wanted to shoot the airplane down. When that failed they continued north after the two girls. Never did they intend for them to escape. For three more hours the men chased them north until they had completely lost their trail in the night.

Dancing Wind fixed the direction of travel with her Garmin G. P. S. and then picked out a star to the north of them. Then Molly and

Dancing Wind continued walking north towards the United States border. Dancing Wind ate her M. R. E. first as they walked, then Molly ate her M. R. E. They would walk through the night.

At midnight the men were exhausted and dropped to the ground to rest and curse their luck that had allowed the teenagers to escape. Both men were suffering from severe lack of water. They removed their shirts to try and cool off. The hot dry desert wind felt good but in actuality it increased their need for water by allowing their sweat to evaporate quicker. Neither man had had a drop of water since about five in the evening when they finished their quart canteens of water then threw them away in the desert.

Poncho told Johnny those girls must have radios to talk to the aircraft. I will bet you the girls deliberately lured us to the north while their friends are back there stealing our gold and silver. It made complete sense to Johnny, as that is what he would also have done. Both men turned to the south to return to their camp and their treasure before the trackers friends came and stole all their gold and silver bullion. First they would surprise and kill the men robbing there camp; then they would go to the United States and find the girls and kill them.

Every fifteen to twenty minutes, the teenagers picked a new star to the north to travel by. Every thirty minutes they rechecked their position on the G. P. S. They walked in silence carefully listening to the sounds of the night. As they walked to the north a small breeze came up from the southwest helping to cool them off. Even without the sun, the temperature was still in the low 90's F. Every fifteen minutes the girls stopped for a minute to rest, and drink water. During their night walk, they would drink every drop from four canteens of water--two gallons. They held their one last canteen in reserve for the next day.

At six in the morning, both teenagers crossed the fence marking the border between the United States and Mexico. They both kissed the ground; they were both so happy to be back, and alive in the United States. Thirty minutes later, out of the east as the sun was rising on a new day, to their surprise, they heard an aircraft flying down low, at five hundred feet above the ground. They smiled at each other, yes it was the Cherokee 140. This was a nice surprise as the teenagers had only paid John for two flights in his aircraft. They had paid him $500 to drop two black bags as they had needed them. Those black bags had made the critical difference in their getting out of the Sonoran Desert alive. Dancing Wind opened her back pack and got out her C. B. radio and transmitted:

"Delta Whiskey to Juliet Mike. '

"Delta Whiskey to Juliet Mike."

Ten minutes later they both climbed aboard the Cherokee and were airborne flying north towards a dirt airstrip outside of Tucson.

★★★★

At six in the morning, Johnny and Poncho woke up to a new day in the Sonoran Desert. For three hours they had been walking towards the south but they were desperate for water. Poncho saw the lake of water to the west of them first. He immediately turned towards the lake he could see about four or five miles away to the west. Johnny looked and saw it too; a wonderful lake full of water, if they could reach it they were saved!

To the west, both men traveled towards the beautiful blue lake of water. It would take hours to get there but the cool refreshing water would be a life saver. Their steps had grown smaller because they were exhausted and suffering from lack of water. It was all they could do to put one foot in front of another and keep traveling.

Johnny was so focused on the lake of water he staggered into the three foot choya cactus he did not see the cactus until he felt the pain from the hundreds of sharp spines. He called to his friend Poncho to come pull the cactus off him, but Poncho continued onward. Poncho knew he needed water. There was no time to help his partner, Johnny would have to take care of himself.

Johnny reached down to pull the cactus off his legs and immediately got two dozen sharp thorns in his hand. Johnny then used his holster to grab the joints of choir cactus thorns off his legs. When most of the thorns were out of his leg Johnny dropped the thorn filled holster on the ground and continued walking westward toward the blue lake carrying his revolver in his hand.

As the temperature climbed to 100 degrees by eleven in the morning, both men knew that their only chance for life depended on reaching the water they saw ahead of them. No longer were the men traveling in a straight line, as they walked both men weaved like a drunken alcoholics. Funny thing, the lake did not seem to be getting any closer. Johnny dropped his revolver and extra ammo to the ground; he would come back for them later after he got water.

Poncho did not want to drop his revolver and ammo but he realized Johnny was right. He just could not haul the extra weight right now. He regretted that he had thrown his canteen away yesterday as he would need to fill his canteen when he reached the lake. Now he had nothing to hold water in. Well that was one mistake he would never make again.

At one in the afternoon, Poncho saw the lake one hundred yards ahead of him. Poncho staggered forward. He had made it to the beautiful blue lake of water in the Sonoran desert. As he walked to the shore and fell to his knees to have a drink, the lake suddenly disappeared! It had been a mirage. Poncho scooped up a handful of water to drink, but all his hands scooped up was sand. "NO! " Poncho croaked. There was simply no energy left for a scream. Poncho took off his shirt, and paints and shoes to cool off from the desert heat as he walked out into the center of his desert mirage. He began digging with his bare hands; he knew the water was here. All he found as he dug was sand.

Johnny followed Poncho out into the mirage. He too scooped up the sand to drink. It can't be. He was so close to being rich. If it was not for those damn teenagers, he would have never have walked out into this GOD forsaken desert. It was their entire fault he was here. As Johnny looked up he saw the black buzzards circling overhead. Oh GOD, he thought he did not want the buzzards to eat him! As a dozen buzzards circled overhead they thanked GOD for dinner. GOD always provided for the birds for he knew their need too.

Two angels stood near the two men. They had done their best to watch over them from the day they were born. Today both Angels thought they would be taking the spirits of Poncho and Juan *home*. The less experienced Guardian Angel turned to the wiser Guardian Angel and asked, "How are we going to get them to go *home* with us? "

The wiser and more experienced Angel replied, "It is as simple as water."

"You mean we baptize them with water? "

"No, just watch."

As Ponchos spirit rose up out of his lifeless body the wiser Angel motioned him to come over to him. He stood one step in front of a door of light. In his hand he held a glass of water.

As Poncho's spirit flew towards the Angel, the Angel simply took two steps back so he was inside the door of light.

As Poncho flew towards the Angel holding the glass of water he flew right into the tunnel of light, and so he flew *home*, just as the Angel intended.

So the second Guardian Angel just copied the wiser Angel's idea and he too took Johnny *home*.

Then the two Angels on each side of the Tunnel of Light entered the tunnel, and then the tunnel disappeared as quickly as it had appeared.

★★★★

After landing at his house, John drove both women to Tucson and rented them a room at the Motel 6. When both women finished their showers and got dressed, John would be taking them out to dinner. After Dancing Wind and Molly had gotten ready for a dinner, they hopped into John McGregor's truck and headed for a nice steak house called the Rustlers Hideout. Here they got a quiet booth by themselves as the dinner crowd had not arrived yet. John wanted to know the whole story about their last three days in Mexico. The teenagers each told bits and pieces of the story between mouthfuls of rare steak they were enjoying. John hung onto every word and interrupted often asking questions.

They told John that they would not be here now if it was not for his help. They asked John if he would he like to accompany them to San Francisco where they planned to sell their gold. What the teenagers told him was that they planned to give twenty-five percent to charity and split the remainder equally. They would each receive an equal share of twenty-five percent of the total. John was enjoying this dinner more and more. Molly told John that she figured that they had eighteen pounds of gold which could be sold for spot. With twelve troy ounces to a pound and eighteen pounds of metal that would come to 216 ounces. At $550 per troy ounce that is $118,800. With $118,800 divided into four equal shares that is $ 29,700 each.

They made two phone calls and they had an appointment at a major bank in three days. Within fifteen minutes of entering the San Francisco Bank they entered a private office where they handed over the three bars of Spanish gold. They left with $118,800 in US currency.

Down on Mission Street at the Salvation Army they made a $29,700 donation to a food kitchen. They escorted the manager to the bank with their donation, then returned him to the food kitchen.

Two hours later they were heading east towards Arizona. Each of them had a year's pay in their pocket. John McGregor told them if they ever wanted some help again just give him a call and he would be there for them. Both teenagers told him that there were numerous jobs where they could use a helping hand.

As John drove his pickup truck east across the Lower California Desert after leaving Barstow, Dancing Wind kept noticing John kept glancing at Molly and her. Dancing Wind knew that John McGregor had a question on his mind. Finally Dancing Wind just turned to John and told him, "Shoot. Go ahead and ask your question."

John told them "I know that it is impossible to track a trail that is two or three hundred years old. I have fought in wars and tried tracking the enemy soldiers, and I know that the trail gets harder and harder to read as it gets older. As time passes the wind, rain, and even time as well as the passage of other people and animals makes the original trail harder and more difficult to read. I know that it is impossible to track a trail that is a year old much less three hundred years old. Yet I have $29,700 on me now that says that somehow you were able to track that trail. I just do not understand how that is possible."

Dancing Wind told John, "Basically what you say is true; but there are three factors that you at present do not understand and did not consider."

"First the trail we followed in the Sonoran Desert had stone trail and cache markers erected by the Jesuits about three centuries ago. Most of these stone markers were still there to help us track the trail. Literally we followed the stone markers the Jesuits had erected. '

"Second the Jesuits intended that their markers and codes would be understood by other Jesuits who might come along years later and recover the cache. The Jesuits who hid the treasure or placed the cache intended that someday the cache would be recovered. We probably understand about half of the Jesuits codes and the Indian sign language that they used three hundred years ago. That is the idea behind the stone markers and the hieroglyphs. '

"Third, we would have never recovered anything nor lived to be here now talking with you if we did not have the help and constant communication with our Guardian Angels! It was only by our listening to our Guardian Angels and following their advice that we were able to recover the cache as we did."

★★★★

Deep unshored trenches and holes are dangerous; they can cave in suddenly with no warning. Four days later the weight of a thousand pounds on the edge of the hole that was dug in the ground caused the west side of the hole to collapse dumping the bars of gold, silver and the wooden tripod back into the hole where the Jesuit priest had placed the bullion three centuries earlier.

★★★★

A week later Juan returned to the small mountain herding his goats. He was very careful approaching the pickup truck with the four flat tires. Strangely no one was around. Two weeks later someone stole the engine.

Another week passed before Juan took the knife from his mother's kitchen. Juan carefully cut the rubber around the trucks front and back windows. Next he removed the side windows from the truck cab. His mother would finally have real glass windows in their house.

The following week his sister helped Juan make the adobe bricks. After the mud and straw bricks dried in the sun, they worked together using the four truck windows and the adobe bricks to give their house real glass windows in the living room and kitchen.

Another three years would pass before Juan would use the bowline and prusik knot for climbing. Juan was curious about the hole up on the mountain where he grazed his goats. He had first seen the hole on his mountain about two weeks after he had the visit from the Indian girl whom had taught him how to tie two knots. Juan's Guardian Angel would be climbing the rope with his charge.

Dearest Beloved
There is no reason
To worry or fear
For do you not know
Your Angels are here!

Wild Buffalo

On the great plains of the western United States there used to roam vast herds of wild buffalo. These majestic bison stood five to six foot tall, and were power houses of stored energy, which occasionally was released when the buffalo stampeded or attacked their enemies such as man trying to hunt and kill them or protect themselves from dangerous predators like wolves. The buffalo provided essential food; tools from their bones, and their hides provided material for tipis, blankets, and clothing for the Native American Indians. Should a fight occur between a domestic animal like cattle and a buffalo, smart money should be placed on the wild buffalo. Buffalo are much more dangerous that domestic cattle.

Wild Buffalo was the name of a Lakota medicine man and respected warrior. He was always trying to help his people through both healing the sick as well as feeding the hungry or less fortunate members of his tribe. He was called Wild Buffalo because he was an extremely strong warrior. As there were no pressing needs to keep him in the village, he rode south with a small band of Lakota Indians to gather a few herbs while elk hunting in Wyoming.

In the spring of 1680, Spanish slave traders captured a group of Lakota Indians camped in the Wind River Mountain Range in western Wyoming. The leader of this small group of Indians was Wild Buffalo. The slave traders sold the Lakota Indians to Spaniards at the Taos Slave Fair. The Spaniards needed more slaves to work in their three gold mines on Taos Mountain. They constantly needed a never ending supply of new slaves due to the high death rate which occurred due to dangerous working conditions and malnutrition. The Spaniards simply worked their slaves to death in their greed to extract more and more gold out of the mines they operated.

Up on Taos Mountain the Spaniards operated three gold mines. Two of these mines were a little over halfway up on the east side of Taos Mountain. The third gold mine was on the north side of the mountain much higher up above 10,000 in elevation. This mine was the most remote of the Taos mines the Spanish miners worked above Taos Pueblo. Here the air was thin, the food was scarce and the life of a slave was measured in months. When one slave died it just meant the Spaniards had to kidnap another Indian and force him in to slavery. If the Indian did not comply with the orders, food was withheld, he was placed in chains, and they would be beaten with a whip. The Spaniards were cruel masters who were ruthless in their treatment of the slaves.

The Spaniards who purchased Wild Buffalo thought they had gotten a great bargain in purchasing the Lakota warrior as he was so strong that he could do the work of two slaves. Because the Lakota warrior was so strong, they quickly called him Bull after the strong bulls found in a herd of cattle. Bull was a quick learner and a couple lashes of the whip and he instantly recognized the new name the Spanish miners called him. Very soon he learned mining, as well as how to pack the pair of panniers (bags) on the pack saddles and load them full of gold to haul off Taos Mountain and down to the town of Valdez located to the west of Taos Mountain. Here the Rio Hondo flowed down to the Rio Grande to the west. The Rio Grande then flowed south down the entire length of New Mexico to the Texas and Mexican border and on out to the Gulf of Mexico.

Occasionally he led the pack mules of gold off Taos Mountain and hauled the gold to Valdez. Sometimes the pack trains of gold were hauled down to where the Rio Hondo flowed into the Rio Grande; near what is now called the Dun Bridge. On rare occasions he would move the mules loaded with gold as far south as the hot springs on the Old Spanish Trail to what are now called the Stage Coach Hot Springs. Along this two mile stretch of the Rio Grande River on the steep gorge cliffs was located "The Cave of Gold of the Rio Grande." Here the Spaniards stored the gold mined from the rich gold mines up on Taos Mountain. Wild Buffalo or Bull as the Spanish slave owners called him learned all he could about the Spaniards and their customs. As a Lakota warrior he made it his duty to learn about his enemies. Wild Buffalo intended to live as a free warrior or die fighting his enemies. He observed that the Spaniards had a lust for gold. These men would lie, cheat, kidnap his people, and even murder to obtain the yellow metal. Nothing was more important to the Spanish conquistadors than gold!

So Wild Buffalo decided the best way to hurt his enemies was to steal as much yellow metal from the Spaniards as possible. Once a month he took twelve mule loads of gold from the mines down to the "Cave of Gold of the Rio Grande". He formulated a plan to kill his enemies and steal all the gold the Indian slaves had been forced to mine that month. He would steal all twelve mule loads of gold!

When Wild Buffalo spoke with the other Indian slaves about all working together to escape with him, he found that most of the Indians would not help him at all! They were more afraid of the beating by the whip than the prospect of dying within a couple of months as slaves mining gold for the Spaniards. Four other Lakota and one Cheyenne Indian slaves would join him in his rebellion to kill the Spaniards and escape.

Had all the Indians worked together to escape their slave masters, Wild Buffalo was sure that the Spaniards could be driven from the land. But with so many Indians scared of their masters or actively working with the Spaniards to track down any Indian who tried to escape, Wild Buffalo realized that within hours of their escape that the other Indians would warn the Spaniards of their escape and even help the Spaniards track them down and capture them. Then the Spaniards would make an example of them cutting off their feet, hanging them from trees or post and whipping them to death or whatever manner of torture they could devise.

It would have been easy had the Indians cooperated and worked together to drive the hated Spaniards from their land. Instead of a few Indians fleeing with a dozen Spaniards chasing them, Wild Buffalo argued that if all the Indians attacked the Spaniards they could easily drive them out of their land. There were over a hundred Indians living in New Mexico for every five Spaniards. If the Spaniards were driven from their land then none of them would be slaves any longer, they would all be free men. While the other Indians agreed with his idea of driving the Spaniards from their land they simply thought it was impossible to refuse to obey the Spaniards whom had enslaved them.

Several hundred feet from the mine entrance was a shrine there the Indians were to pray for their salvation each day before work began. The Indians would say the prayers even though they did not know the meaning of the words, as they would be beaten with a whip if they failed to say the prayers. If the Indians said a prayer to the Great Spirit, or tried to practice their native religion they would be beaten for that too. The padres and Spanish guards told them the way to salvation was the hard work of mining gold for them and saying their prayers. They really wanted nothing to do with the Roman Catholic religion which was beaten into them.

The escape began due to simple exhaustion; which caused one of the Lakota warriors to trip with the load of gold ore he was hauling out of the mine shaft. As the Lakota Indian tripped, he lost his balance. He collided with one of the three Spaniards guarding the Indians at the mine. The load of gold ore collided and fell into one of the guards. Losing his temper, the Spaniard took his spear and drove it into the back of the Lakota Indian killing him.

Wild Buffalo was behind his friend also carrying a bag of gold ore. But instead of fifty pounds of rock in his bag, he was forced to carry twice as much-- a hundred pounds. When Wild Buffalo saw his friend murdered, he lost his temper. With all the force an enraged warrior can muster, he threw the bag with one hundred pounds of rock into the Spaniard who murdered his friend, knocking him off his feet and sending him sprawling. Then pulling the steel tipped spear out of his friend's back, he pivoted and with all the force of a charging warrior, he ran the spear through the armor chest plate of the Spaniard drawing his sword to slay Wild Buffalo.

The Spaniard was slammed into the rock wall; the spear had gone right through his armor. He thought, "This cannot be happening to me." The Indian he called Bull had run his spear through his armor and right through his chest before he could slay him with his sword. As his legs buckled, he felt the Indian pull the sword from his right hand.

Wild Buffalo then used the sword to kill the Spaniard who had murdered his friend. As the Indians poured out of the mine they grabbed the remaining guard, and he died in a short swift fight.

Half of the Indians simply sat down on the ground; they had no idea what to do or where to go. Most of the remaining Indians fled in different directions, telling the story of how the Lakota warrior killed two Spaniards even running the spear through his armor of his breast plate.

Even today on the Taos Pueblo, the elders may speak of the Spaniard high up on the north slope of Taos Mountain with the steel tipped spear sticking out of his steel breast plate. About seventy years ago, the warriors returned to this ancient mine site to close up its entrance when a snow slide had opened it up.

Wild Buffalo directed the three remaining Lakota warriors to help him saddle and load the pack mules. When the pack saddles were in place, and all the mules bridled and a lead line was run between them in three groups of four mules each, they loaded the panniers with two, fifty pounds of gold bars in each pair of panniers. Then they took the gold objects the priest had forced them to make from the small prayer shrine. These were added to the load on the pack mules. When the pack string was loaded, they had two hundred and fifty pounds of gold on each mule. As the pack string left the remote mine the Lakota warriors left taking with them a dozen mules and 3,000 pounds of gold!

Wild Buffalo led the warriors accompanying him north and then east down out of the mountains as they followed the pack trail along the Rio Hondo. They would have a day head start on the Spaniards who would come after them tomorrow. Near Valdez, the warriors saw a lot of cut dry vigas (logs) used for making the roof of the adobe houses.

The eight pack saddles were removed from the mules along with the 3,000 pounds of gold in the panniers. Next half of the pack saddles with their long leather straps were used to strap the dry vigas together to make three rafts to float the gold down the Rio Hondo into the Rio Grande. By floating the gold down the river, the Lakota warriors knew they would not leave any track that could be followed.

While Wild Buffalo assisted two of the warriors lashing together the logs to make three log rafts, he sent the youngest warrior armed with a spear over to the Spanish mission to collect any gold and artifacts there. Wild Buffalo did not want the padres to profit from the gold the Indians had been forced to mine, so he collected the gold from the small church. This additional gold and a few church artifacts, about four hundred pounds, would all be hidden.

Wild Buffalo then asked one of the youngest Lakota warriors, Strong Bear to load the remaining four pack saddles, eight of the panniers with rocks so the mules would look like they were loaded down with gold. He was to take off for the Wind River Mountain Range in Montana and if the Great Spirit would accompany him he could return to his family. His job was to take off north leading the Spanish who would pursue them off in the opposite direction they were traveling. They thanked their brother. They told him to drop the pack saddles and the load of rock as soon as he saw a group of men pursuing him. Then he was to ride like the wind until he reached the safety of a large Lakota village.

Hopefully they would not chase him further after they learned his panniers were simply loaded with ordinary rock. They wished their brother Strong Bear luck and he took the mules and headed north on the Rainbow Trade Trail towards Colorado. They would never see each other again. His job was to decoy the Spanish pursuing them; leading them to the north.

Wild Buffalo knew that the Spaniards would follow the tracks of the mules. But eventually they would realize that the mules were traveling light and they did not have the gold. Then all the Spaniards would pursue him, because they would want all the gold back!

Wild Buffalo planned to hide the gold where no one would ever find it. Nothing would really get the Spaniards as furious as losing their gold. But to hide the gold, he first had to travel without leaving any tracks. That is why he had sent the mules north while he moved the gold south on the Rio Grande. He wanted to leave no tracks and buy himself time to bury the gold where the Spaniards would never find it.

Through the night the three Indian warriors, Wild Buffalo, Fast Runner and Red Fox drifted down the Rio Hondo and into the Rio Grande. Some of the gold bars were lost as they traveled down the two rivers. The Indians did not mind, they had no need for gold. They just wanted to be sure that the Spaniards would never find it.

Wild Buffalo had the perfect hiding place in mind-- right under the noses of the Spanish guards guarding the "Cave of Gold of the Rio Grande". Never would the Spanish think to look near their own guard post. Near the biggest cache of gold bars in northern New Mexico, he would hide the gold. During the night more than 3,000 pounds of gold bullion and church artifacts were concealed in large and small caches in the mud along the river as well as all along the cliff face of the Rio Grande Gorge.

After hiding the gold bullion Wild Buffalo and the two Lakota warriors who were helping him, immediately began to make bows, arrows, and strings so they would have a weapon for self defense from the Spaniards and for hunting game for food. Before they had completed making the bows and their strings, they were captured by the Spanish guards out looking for them. Wild Buffalo, Fast Runner and Red Fox were caught because some of their Indian brothers betrayed them and led the Spanish to them.

Above the Stage Coach Hot Springs, on the east cliffs, is a massacre site where the Spaniards slaughtered over two hundred Indians who did not appreciate being slaves to the Spanish. It was here that the Spaniards tortured and slaughtered the three Indian warriors in July 1680. Never did the Spaniards recover a single bar of gold that Wild Buffalo took from them. Sometimes men can act on an idea or concept like obtaining their freedom. Sometimes they need an example to inspire them and mobilize them into action. Often they need a leader.

A month later, inspired by the Lakota warrior's example, on August 11, 1680, the Indian Rebellion occurred. All the Indian pueblos united as one force to drive the Spanish out of New Mexico. The rebellion or freedom fight began in the Taos Pueblo and swept across all of New Mexico. Popay, an Indian, not of the Taos Pueblo, possibly a Lakota, led the fight for freedom. He told the story to the tribal elders of many pueblos; how one Lakota warrior killed two Spanish conquistadors, then took all the gold from them. It just may be that is what finally spurred them into action was the inspiration and example of a Lakota warrior called Wild Buffalo who died fighting for freedom thirty days earlier.

★★★★

For one week in July of 2004, if one were up early at daybreak on the east side of the Rio Grande Gorge, you might have seen a Lakota Medicine man, facing east praying to the Great Spirit. Beside the Lakota Warrior was an Arapahoe. The Arapahoe was just beginning her education learning Spiritual matters. The Arapahoe's name was Dancing Wind. The Lakota Medicine man was praying in a medicine wheel just to the east of where the Spaniards had slaughtered his brothers 324 years earlier. He was here to ask the Great Spirit and his Angels to help take his brothers home. The Medicine man's spirit name was Wild Buffalo.

When the task at hand
Seems too hard to do
Ask YOUR Angel
To help you!

The Life and Lessons of Barton

As one goes through Barton's life lessons or YOURS, there are five major concepts you must always keep in mind: **First, you are creating your life events!** You chose to be here and experience a series of life lessons. **Second, your thoughts and actions are creative**. Literally your thoughts and actions, or lack of action, set into motion the events you experience. **Third, you will keep repeating the lessons or events in your life until you fully understand the lesson.** If, for example, you need lessons in taking care of your car; you will be repairing a lot of flat tires alongside the road until you learn to not drive your car with very little tread on your tire or the wire cord showing after you have driven your rubber tire far past when you should have replaced it! If you need a lesson in replacing your car battery when it does not want to crank the starter any longer, or you need a lesson in maintaining your cars belts or radiator hoses your car can help you learn the lessons you feel you need to learn. Yes, you created the car you have in your life now. YOU literally set into motion a chain of events: Thoughts followed by action, which resulted in the car you drive now! *If you never thought of owning a car and you never acted on that thought, you would not have a car in your life right now!*

The fourth rule is that: *Like attracts like*. What this means, in brief, is that similar interest or common interest attract people of similar or common interest. Police are most comfortable associating with other police. Airplane pilots will associate with other airplane pilots. Soldiers will associate with other soldiers. Thieves will associate with other thieves. Seaman will associate with other seaman. Prospectors like to hang out with other prospectors. And yes, trackers enjoy hanging out with other trackers.

The fifth rule is called *karma*. Literally, what comes around, goes around. If you do good all the time, good things will tend to happen to you. If you steal from others then others will steal from you. This law shows up a lot in my prospecting and tracking adventures. Often outlaws steal from stagecoaches, trains, and anyone else they can. When outlaws are caught up in the Law of Karma, they are usually caught by the sheriff and the stolen loot is recovered. Alternatively, they lose the loot by burying it and they never get to spend a penny of their stolen loot. When the stolen loot is buried, that is where our spirit tracking comes into play-- with our tracking the outlaws trail and trying to recover the stolen loot. When Dancing Wind is tracking outlaws coming from California in the late 1800's she tracks them to the Stolen meyer River where they were wiped out by Ute Indians. In simple terms, their Karma caught up with them. First, they murdered and stole from people in California, and then they stole food and burned down a Ute Indian encampment. The Ute War party sent after them caught up with the outlaws on the Stollsteimer River wiping out the outlaws and so everything the outlaws stole and murdered to obtain did not do them any good as they lost it all.

LESSON: PLANTING TREES

When I was about five years old I remember my dad taking me to a hardware store in Dayton, Ohio where he selected some fruit trees. He did not just grab any fruit trees but he selected the fruit he liked best. My father purchased apples, pears and a peach tree for me, because I like eating peaches a lot. Then he examined the trees to select the healthiest trees. He wanted a sturdy main trunk without gashes in the bark from mishandling during shipment He liked to see green leaves on the fruit tree. If the leaves were not out yet then my dad would look at the small branches, as he liked to see a green color in the bark of the little 1/8-1/4 inch small branches. If the small branches were brown, broken or when broken they were dry and brittle he would not select that tree. Good trees also have a healthy look to the small buds on the branches. If the buds were all brown and crumbly, when you handled or rubbed them between your fingers then the tree would not be very healthy. Then my dad purchased the fruit trees he selected.

Then out in our yard we dug a big hole for each tree, spreading out the roots throughout the hole. Then we filled the hole with lots of water and while holding the tree upright at its base, we would fill in the entire hole with dirt. By having the hole full of water, it watered the roots, and prevented air pockets from being formed around the roots. Next we refilled the hole with dirt. The hole full of water helped the soil pack firmly around the roots of the fruit tree.

WHAT I LEARNED FROM PLANTING TREES
WITH MY DAD

When a parent teaches a child about planting trees, the lesson can be remembered long after the child's parent has gone *home* in spirit. Certainly I remember doing this with my dad about fifty years ago. I guess this lesson is still with me as I am still planting trees more than 20,000 trees later! And yes, I still remember my dad teaching me how to select the best fruit trees, even though I was very little. I still prefer to plant fruit trees, but over the years I have also planted a lot of pine trees, raspberries, asparagus, garlic, dry land grass and wild rice seed. I feel that it is more important than ever to try and help Mother Earth. The earth is being recklessly destroyed by man. Unless we change our behavior, human kind will not be able to live on this planet much longer. It is our privilege and responsibility to care for Mother Earth. Each individual effort to protect and preserve our planet makes a difference.

LESSON: BULLIES

I can remember being attacked three times in school by bullies. So far as I can recall, nothing was done to punish the individuals who attacked me. The first attack occurred in a classroom that the teacher had left. As I was walking to my desk my arms were grabbed and held behind my back while the second person repeatedly punched me in the stomach. They released me when the attack was over, and I collapsed to the floor. When I could get up, I walked home and never wanted to go back to school. My parents forced me to return to school. The second attack was on the school playground. I only recall that I was beaten up. The third attack was in the school hallway. As I was walking down the hall I was struck by a teenager with a wooden club. He thoroughly beat me up very badly in about ninety seconds by repeatedly striking me with his wooden club.

WHAT I LEARNED: FROM THE ATTACK

After the third time that I was beaten up, I decided to learn Korean Karate (Tae Kwon Do). I took the karate classes to learn how to protect myself. Another lesson I learned was that many times one is attacked or assaulted without any provocation on your part. Some people are mean or evil and they look for weaker victims to attack, torment, or rob. Over the years, looking back, I have always felt the time, money and effort to learn karate were well worth it. Later in life this lesson will return several more times. Do you think the outcome will be the same? Or have I learned this lesson well enough so I can quit repeating it. Have you also experienced this lesson in your life?

LESSON: BEING CHEATED ON THE MONEY WE HAVE EARNED OR CHEATED ON THE LABOR WE HAVE PERFORMED

Lesson three grew out of lesson two. Because of lesson two (attacks by bullies), I decided to take a Korean Karate classes. As my parents were opposed to my taking karate classes, they would not provide any financial help paying for the classes. To pay for the classes I got a job working at Kentucky Fried Chicken. There I learned a lesson involving money. They paid me $1. 35 per hour for working from 4 pm to 10 pm when the restaurant closed. Then the manager punched out all his employees on the time clock when the restaurant closed. Then the rest of the employees and I worked on average two more hours cleaning the restaurant, sweeping and mopping the floors as well as cleaning the restrooms. The employees were kept busy removing the trash, cleaning the grills, cleaning the stock /supply room scrubbing pots and pans, removing grease and generally making the restaurant spotless for the next day of operation. The restaurant paid us employees for 5. 5 hours work each day, as they deducted 30 minutes to eat. All of us put in 7. 5 hours of work so the restaurant chain cheated us on two hours of labor every day. All of us put up with being cheated on each paycheck as we all needed the job.

Another one of the lessons that I learned is that money brings out dishonesty in many individuals. Simply stated many people will cheat you if they can. I put up with this to get the money to pay for my karate lessons. Because I have tolerated being cheated on wages/ money owed me-- as did all the other employees-- we all will have to repeat this lesson again and again until we learn the solution to this problem. Each of us working at the restaurant created the lessons we encountered there. It is through learning one's lessons that one can then advance to learn the next lesson. Or if you did not learn your lesson you can repeat it as many times as needed throughout your life. For most of us, lessons like being cheated of our money or cheated on the labor we perform are not pleasant lessons that we like to repeat very often!

LESSON: THE GARDEN RAKE

When I was a teenager garden rakes were used to rake up leaves, weeds and work in the garden. One day as I was working out in the lawn I stepped on the garden rake and the sharp pointed tines went right into my foot. The pain was intense, the bleeding was minor, my foot was sore for weeks while it healed. The lesson lasted a life time! I learned to always put the rake away when not in use. Most important of all is to always leave the rake with the pointed tines pointing into the earth, so if you accidently step on the rake no harm will befall you.

LESSON: CHOOSING FRIENDS

When I was in high school I had a friend who was involved in organized crime. We used to go hunting, fishing, shooting, flying, and scuba diving. I was interested in listening to his stories concerning organized crime. We would jump in his car and go for a drive where he would show me where bootlegger operations occurred during Prohibition. In downtown Baltimore, he would show me where a bakery was located that sold bootleg whiskey in the backroom.

On one such drive, he pointed out a street corner and told me about three men who once stood there. A car drove up and then a gunman assassinated the man on the left and the right leaving the center man alive. When the police and newspaper reporters showed up, the sole surviving witness said he did not see anything; but he knew the men on his left and right were killed by a professional assassin. The reporter then asked, if he did not see anything at all, how he knew that the other men were murdered by a professional assassin. He replied that an amateur would have killed all three of us. A professional assassin would just kill the targets he was paid to murder.

There were many interesting stories about prohibition. Because alcohol was illegal, alcohol was very expensive. This attracted organized crime because the criminals knew selling illegal alcohol would lead to fast cash profits. In ships off shore, and down in the Bahamas, small high speed boats called rum runners transported cases of alcohol from the ships or the Bahamas to the United States mainland. Literally these small high speed boats called rum runners were smuggling alcohol into the United States.

To increase their profits, many smugglers started cutting the alcohol with water. One rum runner named McCoy would not cut his whiskey with water like the less honest smugglers had done to increase their profits. Whenever a boat load of alcohol arrived from McCoy, you could be sure it was the real thing or the genuine article. In bars, customers would ask who brought in this good whiskey and they were told it was McCoy's whiskey. Soon all up and down the Atlantic coast, customers began asking for McCoy's whiskey as it was not cut with water. If the drink in the bar was watered down, often the customer would say: *"Give me the real McCoy"*. Over the years then the expression came down that *"The Real McCoy"* means the real thing or the genuine article.

A more modern smuggler may use a helicopter to pick up packages off shore in the Atlantic Ocean. The helicopter will fly to the site where smugglers have dropped off packages for pickup. The vessel which drops off the package at the agreed upon rendezvous point, will pack the smuggled goods in a watertight steel containers. This container is weighted down with lead so it sinks to the bottom of the ocean. Attached to the outside of the container will be a buoy which will pop to the surface of the ocean when it receives an electronic signal. When the helicopter flies out to the drop off site, they will use an electronic device like a garage door opener which will tell the buoy to float to the surface of the ocean. Then the package of smuggled goods is picked up by the helicopter using a hook on the skid to grab the buoy. A skilled helicopter pilot can pick up a package of smuggled goods in 60-90 seconds!

This federal agent Mark had told his wife Sam that she was never to buy stolen property. Mark had explained to Sam that no matter how great the bargain on the stolen goods she would put him in an embarrassing position if she were to be arrested for purchasing stolen property. Well, Sam just could not help herself when at the grocery store parking lot a truck full of seafood pulled up and two men began selling all the boxes of seafood at $5 each! Sam just could not resist buying two five pound boxes of breaded shrimp for $10 even though she knew that they were stolen. She got home with the shrimp and put them on the stove in a skillet with some oil to fry the breaded shrimp. Then she went to do the laundry.

As Mark arrived home from work and walked in the door of his house, he could smell and see that the shrimp on the kitchen stove had caught fire. He immediately grabbed the skillet and threw it and its burning contents out in the back yard. Mark asked his wife what she was doing and she told him washing the clothes. Mark told Sam that she should have been watching the shrimp she was cooking. Sam told Mark it was not her fault that the shrimp caught fire. What did he expect with "hot shrimp" (stolen shrimp.)Sam told Mark that she had learned her lesson about buying "hot shrimp", but since dinner was burned she would get dressed so he could take her out to dinner!

Almost all the stories I was told were of the old days. Once I was told a story about a weapons shipment that came out of Japan. This was a shipment of modern weapons which was abandoned at a cache site on federal property as the smugglers could clearly see numerous federal law enforcement agents in plain sight looking towards them. As they could see the federal agents they assumed that the federal agents could see them. I do not think the federal agents had their light bulbs on (they were not thinking), as they were not recognizing the illegal activity that they saw on their home turf.

I was told that I could use the information to collect a reward then bounce back a kickback (a large sum of money). But I was told, "The buck stops with you." I wrote a letter to the Federal Alcohol Tobacco and Firearms about getting a reward for the location of a shipment of weapons. Before mailing the letter, two men examined the letter and clarified certain points with me. Then I mailed the letter I had typed to the Alcohol, Tobacco and Firearms. The federal agent who came and saw me wanted the location of the weapons and he told me he would get me fired from my job if I did not give him everything he asked for. His threat to have me fired was made on Monday and on Friday I was fired from where I worked. Next the threats escalated with his threatening to kill me over a dozen times if I did not get him the information promptly. It became clear, very rapidly, that the federal agent had no dignity, no honor, no integrity and no intention of giving or paying any reward! Simply stated he had less integrity, honor, trust, and respect than any individual I had ever encountered!

Had I been honestly paid I was fully prepared to give the federal officers a series of numbers representing the exact coordinates. But that is all I was prepared or willing to put on the table. They wanted names, dates, places literally everything I knew, and as I told the individuals who had told me the story: "The buck will stop with me." Fortunately, during numerous conversations with the Alcohol, Tobacco, and Firearms, I never gave them any data that they continually fished for. Naively I never suspected treachery from the federal government!

Shortly thereafter, the federal agents served me with a subpoena to appear before a grand jury. Now before I was to appear, both parties came and spoke with me. The individuals who told me the story asked me what I was going to say. I told them: "The buck stops here with me". The federal agents also prepped me for my visit to the Grand Jury telling me that if I did not provide them with everything they wanted that they would spread the word everywhere that I was an informant and if that did not get me killed, they would kill me and no one would ever investigate a federal officer doing a hit on me!

I appeared before a grand jury in Baltimore and I was questioned by XXXX XXXX, an assistant U. S. Attorney. They questioned me for several hours. Did I write the letter? Yes. Did I deny anything I said: No, of course not (I did not want to be caught in a lie in case they had taped any conversations.)Had they played tapes of all our conversations, the Grand Jury should have indicted its Federal Officers working in the court house building. But I knew that would never happen. I explained I got the information from an Ouija board and dowsing, and I would be happy to work, getting the location of the weapons as soon as they paid me. How did I know that the weapons were manufactured by Charles Baily? Let's see. The weapons were either manufactured by Charles Baily or Charles Daily, and I knew that it could not be the one name as the Ouija board had said it was weapons. Wasn't Charles Daily the mayor of New York or Chicago? So I knew that it could not be the mayor's name so it had to be the other name. Had I been pressed further for a location of the weapons, I would have located the U. S. Arsenal at Harper's Ferry. I do not believe this arsenal still exists as it dates back to the time of John Brown wanting to free the slaves and being hung for it.

John Brown was just a man ahead of his time. The U. S. attorney was not very happy with my answers. I kept my word. The buck stopped with me! I did call the federal agent and asked him to return my map that was dowsed for a mineral deposit! I really did know how to dowse a little. Never use an Ouija board, as it can open you up to low level spirits and in time they can get possession of you! Ouija boards are like a one way slide down hill, just like using the drug methamphetamine!

WHAT I LEARNED FROM THIS LESSON ABOUT WHO YOUR FRIENDS ARE AND WHO YOU ASSOCIATE WITH WAS NOTHING!

Literally I did not learn anything! Because I did not learn the lesson about only working with and being with people who demonstrate in their daily life dignity, honor, and keeping their word, I was destined to repeat this lesson again and again. Literally this lesson keeps repeating again and again throughout my life as I did not learn the lesson I was being taught! The lesson that I failed to learn is that: *"Like attracts like."* If you associate with individuals who are dishonest and crooked, you will attract people around you who are dishonest and crooked. I worked for a dishonest individual at a restaurant. I associated with an individual who was not always honest, so I attracted people in my life who were not honest. The dealing with the Alcohol Tobacco and Firearms took working with dishonest and deceitful people to an extreme and still I did not see the lesson that I was supposed to learn! I hope you are not as slow of a learner as I was!

If you associate with dishonest people and you allow them to cheat you, then you will draw in to your life more dishonest people. Just as my employer did not treat his employees with the dignity, the honor, and the honesty that they really deserved, the federal agents I drew towards me also lacked this quality.

Since you are creating the events in your life then if a woman allows a man to batter her and beat her up on a regular basis that is what she wants! It is literally a life lesson she chooses to experience and learn! And if she leaves a man who assaults her, she will be drawn to another man who beats her up until she will no longer tolerate it. When she has learned her lesson, then she will move to a man who treats her with the respect, dignity and honor she and all people deserve.

LESSON: LIKE ATTRACTS LIKE

When I was a teenager, I saw the movie "Valdez is Coming" where the hero in the film used an old fashioned revolver and a Sharps 45-70 rifle. So I wanted a revolver and a Sharps 45-70 rifle. This wish or thought followed by action literally sets into motion the unfolding events. I went to gun shows, checked with gun dealers, all in an effort to own a Sharps 45-70 rifle. In the movie, Valdez (Burt Lancaster) uses a 45-70 rifle to shoot the men trying to kill him. Valdez starts killing the men chasing him at 600 yards. This is an extremely long range to hit a man on a horse. I knew that I could be a good shot if I had a similar rifle. So I put the word out on the street that I was looking for an old Navy revolver and a Sharps rifle. When stories get repeated they often get changed a little. Soon the word was out on the streets that I was an "arms dealer."

Baltimore had a program to get guns off the streets. Using tax payer money, the police department purchased rifles and hand guns. The police paid $50 for each rifle and $100 for each hand gun which they would destroy. In the "Washington Post" I saw a picture of them loading up a police paddy wagon with weapons and taking them to Bethlehem Steel to be melted into steel for use in construction. A lot of individuals did their patriotic duty and turned in their firearms that did not function so they could use the money to buy new reliable firearms.

One day, some police men in uniform came from Baltimore to see me. The word on the street that they had heard was I was an "arms dealer." They had hundreds of firearms to sell me. They told me they had gone through the firearms that they were escorting to be melted down into raw steel and selected the very best of the firearms. They wanted to sell me those weapons in lots of a hundred. They told me they could supply me with all the weapons I wanted! I politely told them I appreciated them taking the time to come see me but the story on the street, as stories often do had gotten changed by word of mouth. I was interested in buying firearms but I was only interested in old black powder revolvers and the Sharps 45-70 rifle.

WHAT I LEARNED IN THE LIKE ATTRACTS LIKE LESSON WAS NOTHING!

Literally nothing! Again in my life this lesson will return again and again until I do learn it. I was like a kid playing with fire and I had not yet got burned enough to learn my lesson. What I should have learned was that when you associate with dishonest men you will attract dishonest men into your life.

LESSON: LIKE ATTRACTS LIKE: A NIGHT DIVE.

One night I was visiting a friend. A hurricane was coming up towards Maryland. There was a cargo vessel with its cargo of smuggled goods which was running for shelter trying to avoid the high wind and seas. A line had been swept overboard and gotten sucked into the propeller and shaft, jamming them up tight. They needed a diver NOW! So we loaded up our dive gear and drove to a pier where a fast launch was waiting to take us out to sea. We loaded our equipment on board the boat then left the shelter of the harbor headed for sea. Once we left the shelter of the rock break water, we were in heavy seas.

The bow (front) of the launch was about four feet above the water, the stern (back) only two feet. The seas were running eight to twelve feet! I've always liked working with professionals. They always know their stuff and if you pay attention to them you can learn a lot. An amateur in the same situation will get you killed! Handling the launch on the rough seas took a skilled professional helmsman if we were all going to live through the night! If a single wave came over the stern or hit us broadside, our vessel would slip under the waves in an instant and there would be no trace we had ever gone on this journey together to our deaths. Am I exaggerating? Maybe a little, but I have no doubt that an amateur at the helm would have killed most of us very rapidly. I actually thought that a rogue wave two or three times a normal wave, or the rough seas we were experiencing if it hit us broad side or over the stern, would instantly sink us. I also thought that the two divers aboard would be the only ones who could possibly get ashore alive. As one of the divers, I felt that the Poseidon Dry suit that two of us were wearing would protect us from drowning and exposure so as to enable us to have a chance to get ashore alive.

When we reached the vessel, I was to clear the propeller shaft of the rope wound about the propeller and shaft. It was about one in the morning, pitch black outside and the wind was howling through the rigging. Before going over the side of the launch, I put on the aluminum scuba diving tank, a weight belt, facemask, fins, snorkel, two dive knives, an inflatable life vest, compass, and two hand held spot lights. Both the dive knives and hand held spotlights were tied to my body as well as one safety line connecting me to the launch. The weight belt had a quick release on it that I could instantly drop if I got into trouble. A second line connected me to the stern of the vessel that I was going to work on.

The Captain of the vessel gave me some stupid instructions prior to the dive which went in one ear and out the other. He told me not to cut the line tangled around his propeller shaft as it was an expensive gold braded woven line. I then dove into the water and pulled myself on a line over to the vessel I was here to work on. As the vessel was rapidly rising and falling with each passing wave, the boat had slammed down and hit me a couple of times on the head flooding my face mask with water. Repeatedly I had to stop and clear my flooded face mask, holding in on my face mask with one hand and blowing air out my nose to purge my face mask of water, so I could see clearly. I found that the best way to begin cutting the line away from the shaft was to stand with my legs spread apart on the hull bottom with my body being upside down. I held one line which I was cutting in one hand along with the spotlight to allow me to see where I was cutting. In my left hand, I held a knife I was cutting the ropes with, as well as a line holding me to the boat I was working on. When the face mask was knocked askew, and flooded with seawater, I simply cleared it of water, blowing air into the mask with my nose and then resumed working cutting line after line. What could have been done in five minutes on the safety of dry land took me thirty minutes under difficult sea conditions. When I finished my dive work on the vessel, the Captain started and tested his marine engine shifting it into forward and reverse. When he was confident everything was working properly I was hauled aboard the launch and we returned back to the wharf. This was my first night dive!

WHAT I LEARNED IN THE LIKE ATTRACTS LIKE DIVING LESSON

I had learned my skills as a scuba diver well enough that I could do a night dive and work in adverse conditions. Literally this work that night built up my self confidence. The lesson I failed to learn was that if I had not been associating with whom I did; that I would not have been out there risking my life in the first place! I was sixteen years old when I performed this night dive!

LESSON: ATTENDING HIGH SCHOOL

What did I need to learn? Now remember your thoughts and actions are creative. Barton graduated from high school (Even if I hated every moment of it).

THE LESSON I LEARNED IN ATTENDING HIGH SCHOOL

If you work hard to achieve a goal, even if it takes years to accomplish, if you work at it steady and do your best, you can achieve the goal you set for yourself!

LESSON: AT CALHOON ENGINEERING SCHOOL AND WORKING ABOARD LARGE OCEAN GOING MERCHANT SHIPS

I entered Calhoon Engineering School and studied Marine Engineering. One had to study constantly. I believe I learned more in this school in six months than I did in four years of high school because the curriculum was so intense. After six months of school, I was placed on a ship to work.

My first ship was the S. S. Mormack Bay hauling coffee to South America. After weeks at sea we arrived in Recifi, Brazil, I learned why it took eight men to buy bread in Recifi. By selecting eight men to get bread it insured as much as humanly possible that the bread would get back to the ship. I volunteered to accompany the shore party in search of French bread to be used that night for the dinner on the aft deck of the ship. The bread was going to accompany some steaks, sausage, and wine in a relaxing dinner.

Outside the gate the eight of us started to pile into a taxi cab—it was a difficult and bunched up task. We had no sooner started off when a Mercedes Benz car cut in front of our taxi cutting us off. Out jumped a beautiful woman who went running toward us crying out the name of one of the seaman accompanying us. He jump out of the car and ran into her arms. They showered kisses on each other and their arms embraced and kissed. The seaman jumped into the car with the woman and they sped off. The seven of us resumed our journey in search of bread.

At the first street, we arrived at in town, another seaman shouted out the name of a woman he saw walking down the street with her arms full of bags. She looked at us, and then focused her eyes on one seaman. Next she dropped her bags and screamed out his name as she rushed towards our taxi. Our taxi cab pulled over to the curb and the seaman said to us "There are plenty of you to get the bread I'll catch you later," as he ran into the woman's arms. The six of us continued our journey another hundred feet when a similar action was completed!

By the time we had gotten two blocks into the town of Recifi we had lost three men. When we stopped at a bank to exchange our dollars for centavos, the Brazilian currency, we lost another man outside the bank. I did not know a word of the Portuguese language but obviously the seaman knew the language and what to say as he engaged a beautiful woman in a discussion which clearly held both their interest. Two seaman had only accompanied us to the bank to get money. When they got the local currency they told the remaining two of us that they trusted we could get the bread back to the ship. The two of us got back into the taxi and continued our journey.

When we traveled another two blocks, the last seaman accompanying me banged on the door with his hand and yelled for the taxi to stop. The taxi pulled over to the curb and he started out the door! No way was I going to let him get away, and I grabbed him by his shirt and told him he was not going anywhere—until we purchased the bread! The lady he had seen disappeared from sight and reluctantly he accompanied me to the bakery. As we had intended we purchased the bread from the bakery. Once outside the bakery one of his South American wives with her daughter walked up to us. He embraced her in a lover's embrace as he kissed her. He introduced me to his wife and their step-daughter Juanita. He told her he was just getting some groceries and was on the way to her house. Then they invited me for dinner. So I accompanied them as they went shopping for some groceries. The men on the ship could wait a little while for the bread.

Juanita did not speak more than twenty words of English. I did not speak any words of Portuguese. We were able to understand each other perfectly. She knew exactly what was on my mind from the moment I saw her. Before the morning sunrise our clothes were piled on top of each others at the foot of Juanita's bed.

The next morning I got the bread back to the ship. They would then be able to have it for dinner that night. Me? I was going to take Juanita out for dinner.

★★★★★

For the safety of ships at sea, the cargo ships have Plimsoll Marks near the bow of the ship down near the waterline. The Plimsoll Marks are the legally maximum load the ship is allowed to haul for the sea conditions that it is operating in. For example, a ship operating on the North Atlantic Ocean in summer is allowed to load and haul more cargo than in the winter. Much less cargo would be allowed in winter as the sea conditions in the North Atlantic in winter can be very bad. By loading the ship lighter in terms of the cargo she is carrying, the ship is less likely to be sunk by a bad storm at sea.

If a ship is dangerously overloaded then the Plimsoll Marks will be under water. An overloaded ship can make more money as it is hauling more cargo than legally allowed. When the Mormack Bay went to leave South America the Plimsoll marks were under water. So the Chief Mate had the seaman aboard the ship take a cargo container full of cargo and lifts it with the ships boom out over the water on the opposite side of the ship from the dock. So the ship leaned over in the water. The Plimsoll Marks on the side of the container went deeper under water. The Plimsoll Marks on the shore side came out of the water—at least until the container was placed back aboard the ship. This caused the Plimsoll Marks to momentarily come out of the water by a eighth of a inch. Then the captain told all the officers to sign their name in the log book that the ship was not overloaded. The captain had the officers walk to the dock and they all signed their names in the log book that they personally examined the load of the ship at the wharf and the Plimsoll Marks were out of water! People often do what is wrong to keep their job. Even overloading a ship going out to sea!

When we got back to New York and off loaded the cargo of coffee we got paid for the voyage. I had made $600 for a three month voyage. I was rich. I had saved up three months pay while I was at sea and had no place to spend my money.

One seaman, actually an engineer complained to the Shipping Commissioner that he had been shorted $2. 25. The company had given him $3,000 for the voyage. The engineer was owed $ 3,002. 25. They had given him hundred dollar bills—new hundred dollar bills. When the Shipping Commissioner went to count the new money he slowly counted off the hundred dollar bills. When he counted to thirty, the commissioner handed the thirty bills to the seaman. Then the Shipping Commissioner turned to the shipping company officials and handed them back five of the one hundred dollar bills! ! The new money had stuck together and they had accidentally overpaid the seaman five one hundred dollar bills! The shipping officials did have to give the engineer his $2. 25.

The next two ships that I worked on were the American Ace a container ship and the Valley Forge tanker hauling oil and gas. I was especially unhappy on the tanker and I wanted to return home. They fired me from the tanker for wearing hearing protection in the engine room. When I returned to Calhoon Engineering School, they fired me the hour I returned as they had a letter from the ship that fired me that I was insubordinate.

LESSONS I LEARNED AT CALHOON ENGINEERING SCHOOL AND ABOARD THE MERCHANT SHIPS

Now let's look at this in three ways: What did I need to learn? What events were created? What were the lessons that I learned? If I did not learn my lessons then I will keep repeating them!

What I learned has a number of parts: By working on a ship, I thought I would make the money to buy a Skipjack (fishing / sailing vessel)—in fact I did not make any more money on the ship than if I had stayed home.

I enjoyed my first sexual relationship with a woman. But in the end there is much more than sex in a relationship. There is communication—both people in the relationship should be able to talk with each other. They should express their interests, desires, plans, thoughts, and this communication must flow both ways. Common interests, goals, and working together are also important in a relationship. They should understand and taking into consideration the other persons needs. There is Love. Also important are common spiritual interests / understanding. Loyalty is very important. Humor / Smiles make the hard times go so much easier. A willingness to help each other in times of need is important to me. And meeting each other's sexual needs is important too. The more mature the parties and the more common interest that the man and woman have in common, the less the likelihood of a divorce.

The lesson on overloading a ship I had read about in one of Louis L'Amour's books set in the late 1800's about the sea. After seeing it first hand, I know that the practice still continues of overloading merchant ships. When money is involved, honesty often disappears. Come to think about it, this lesson has been repeated very often in my life—it is time I acknowledge this lesson and move on to the next lesson. As this story continues you will find me repeating this lesson again and again. I hope you do not have to repeat this lesson too often!

The lesson the engineer taught me is that before complaining that someone has cheated you of the money you are owed, take the time to count your money twice. I am sure the engineer will never forget the $500 that he was overpaid. His shipmates will help prevent the engineer from forgetting by constantly joking with him about the day he gave away $500 to collect $ 2. 25, and the day he forgot to count his money before opening his mouth to complain.

When I quit holding on to the goal of being on the ship, and I wanted off, then the creative events to remove me from the ship were set into motion. I was fired off the last ship I worked aboard.

LESSON IN SEARCHING FOR MONEY

This lesson begins with my wishing for a fishing boat. The thought of owning my own fishing boat was followed by action. I started looking at boats and began saving money to buy a fishing boat. My brother Rolland told me he would sell me his fishing boat as he was busy with construction. My brother was building houses. So I purchased the fishing boat from my oldest brother for $4,000. Earning $200 a month, this oyster boat represented a lot of work; every penny I made working for twenty months of labor! To understand this, take every penny you make, your gross salary per month, and multiply it by twenty months! It is a good chunk of money. So I began oystering with my oyster boat in the Chesapeake Bay. At the same time I held a part time job with Newport Condominiums as a maintenance man.

Oystering or fishing is very hard work. You are up before sunrise to get your fishing boat out to the fishing grounds by sunrise. You work all day long and head for home about five in the evening. By the time most folks are home enjoying dinner you are arriving at the buy boat to off load and sell your day's catch. While it is common to tell everyone about the large catches you have made. My largest catch was one hundred and twenty bushels of oysters which paid me about $270 for a days' work. I was paid $ 2. 25 for a bushel full of oysters. There are also days when the winds were so high and the seas so rough that I had caught nothing at the end of the day! Worse yet I had to pay twenty dollars out of my pocket to put gas in the boat so I could go fishing the following day! The average I made fishing was $20-30 for a twelve hour day of work. But I liked the work and being on the boats out on the Chesapeake Bay.

A favorite memory of mine is when I purchased this oyster boat from my brother and brought her home from Chrisfield to Annapolis, Maryland. It was a long voyage up the Chesapeake Bay. I really enjoyed that day cruising over the water at the helm of my first fishing boat. It was a very relaxed and self assured feeling that came over me. I would describe the feeling as the feeling one gets when one is with Angels or has just had an enjoyable or moving conversation with an Angel. It was a really wonderful day. In time I decided to sell the fishing boat. I sold the boat and used the money to pay for my college education. I thought that with a good education, I could get a good paying job.

LESSON LEARNED IN SEARCH OF MONEY

This lesson seems to involve not being happy with what you have. Certainly I seem to be pursuing the big money everywhere! I seem to think that the money is in the next job or the next; never being happy with the money I make. I do not think that when I constantly jump from job to job that I really saved any money, nor made more money. Along with this is the lesson you need to be good at what ever job you work at. You should enjoy the work you do, and be as good at your work as possible. This lesson ended with my selling my boat, quitting my job and going off to college in Vermont to get my college degree.

LESSON: ATTENDING COLLEGE

This lesson begins with my attending GODdard College. This was a very expensive college for me. I wanted to learn all I could as I did not know how many semesters of college that I could afford. So I tried to take every class that I could. To give the reader an idea of what my first semester was like I took these classes: Aquatic Biology, Natural Ecology, Nature and Uses of the Forest, Farm Management, Ecological Agriculture, Ecology and Society, Ecology of the Cities, Visiting Faculty Series, and Chemistry of Pollution. I do not recommend that anyone take nine classes in a semester. On Monday, my first class started at 5 a. m. My last class ended at 10 p. m. Then I could start doing my homework. The average class was two hours. The longest classes were four hours.

Because I had to be very frugal to attend college, I had made myself a budget of $20 per month to cover expenses like laundry, soap, meals out, shopping, and all the other college expenses. Some students had budgets of $10 per month, so a visit to the dentist with a toothache was a major financial disaster. Some students had budgets of over $1,000 a month for expenses.

As part of my financial aid package, I had a work study job. I had to spend about eight hours a week as an emergency driver. The eight hours could come at any time, day or night, and often did. To be able to locate me, I had to give the phone operators my schedule of classes and where I would be throughout the day and night. If I went to the library to study, I called the operator that I would be at the library. When I got ready to leave the library, I had to call the operator when I was leaving the library and where I was going. Every day I would follow this procedure throughout the day.

My boss was a woman and we got along like a cat and a dog. If we were in the same room for very long, we would be at each other's throat. I never intended to start an argument with my boss; but she would always make a smart or vicious comment about me and within a few minutes of my entering a room, the gloves came off. There were over a dozen emergency drivers; but very quickly, I was told not to bother coming to the biweekly emergency driver meetings. I was not fired from my job; my boss just felt that the farther I stayed away from her the better. I was always happy to help out my boss in this manner!

I handled about half of all the emergency calls and the bosses' team handled the other half. I believe the reason for this was that I was good about always letting the operators who dispatched us know where to locate me. I would take any student anywhere they needed to be if it was a real medical situation. By anywhere, I mean anywhere! There was a girl who was injured at the college by some student who did not have common sense. This individual at GODdard College strung a clothes line across a bicycle path. At night, the girl was riding her bicycle back to her dorm when she rode into the clothesline which hit her in the face injuring her eyes and throwing her onto the ground! Her family had a doctor fly up to see her and examine her eyes at the Burlington Hospital at night.

I took the college emergency vehicle and drove her about a hundred miles each way to see the eye specialists. I spent about six hours on this night run, because it was the right thing to do! And I hope if the shoe was on the other foot *you* would do it, too. Every time I took an action like this, my boss told me "You went too far; I am going to have to fire you for what you just did! "

Another time, there was a student who had a bad toothache. I *knew* her spending money was $10 a month! When she came and saw me she was crying from the pain in her tooth. I took her to the dentist in the emergency vehicle, because if the shoe was on the other foot I would want someone to help me. I have a lot of respect for that Vermont dentist. The dentist charged her $10 to pull the tooth and another $10 for seven days of antibiotics! I knew that he had adjusted his rate down, way down, to what she could afford! My boss would tell me "You went too far; that is not what the emergency vehicles are for, I cannot keep you on when you abuse the use of the emergency vehicles." In her meeting with the other emergency drivers; my boss would use me as an example of an emergency driver who does everything wrong! I frequently provided my boss with lots of examples of my irresponsible behavior she could use in instructing her dozen emergency drivers; as I handled dozens of emergency calls. I tried to be there for the emergencies when the students really needed my help.

I took drunks to the local hospital as they insisted that someone must have put drugs in their beer. Of course I knew that they could not have any drugs or beer left in their system after they vomited several times all over me! But I took them to the hospital to be on the cautious side. I honestly do not like any one to vomit all over me!

Another student I took to the hospital scared me. I was called to his dorm to take him to the hospital. First I checked that he was breathing. He was not responsive to my voice or touch. Then I went to look into his eyes to see of the pupils were enlarged or contracted. There was no pupils under his eye lids—just pure white. He had a heart beat and shallow breathing. I really wanted help and got some students to help carry him out to the emergency vehicle. Then I grabbed one of the college security officers to drive the vehicle as I wanted to be sure that he continued to breathe. I told the officer to hurry as I was afraid that if we took too long to get to the hospital, we might lose him.

The officer did not just drive fast that night; he literally flew low getting us to the hospital. Several miles before the Burlington hospital is a traffic light and we were intending to run the red light. We were really moving fast. Suddenly on our left we saw a car rapidly approaching the traffic light on a collision course with us. The other car did have the green light. So the officer driving my emergency vehicle slammed on the brakes. I was in the very back of the vehicle giving mouth to mouth resuscitation. I did three complete summersaults and just before I went through the front windshield, the officer who was in a seat belt caught or grabbed me just before my face went through the glass. He asked me if I was alright and I told him: "Hit It! " I wanted to get to the hospital as fast as possible. When we arrived at the emergency entrance to the hospital the officer ran in to get some medical help. I was busy giving mouth to mouth resuscitation to the young man we were transporting to the hospital.

I saw the young man several days later over at his dorm, and I was happy he was doing fine. Certainly the security officer and I had done our best to keep him alive. I guess GOD or his Angels often give a person a second chance. Should I be speaking to you, I certainly hope that you make the most of this opportunity that GOD has given *you!*

College was rough on the students. I saw students become hardcore alcoholics. I saw students who were taken away for their drug use. Others had mental break downs. Just because you went to college, did not mean that you had common sense. I saw students drink so much beer that they went out on the lawn and threw up, then they came back inside and drank even more so they could go out and throw up again! Certainly the student who strung a clothes line across a bicycle path showed poor judgment. The most common problem facing college students was lack of money to pay the tuition. When I think back on college, I think about the fact that only about one in three students made it to graduation.

Once when I was in Chemistry Lab I saw two students passing an open 1,000 ml beaker of sulfuric acid over the heads of other students who were busy writing in their notebooks. Then the student beside me passed a beaker of acid over the head of the student and the chemistry teacher. I stopped my experiment and went over to the student and told him not to pass the open beakers of acid over anyone because if it slipped from his grip or the student raised his head up or got up, the beaker with the sulfuric acid would spill the acid all over them and immediately burn the student badly.

The chemistry teacher saw me giving instructions to another student and grabbed me by the arm and forcefully removed me from the lab. In the hallway he told me to shut up and never give another student instructions in chemistry, is that clear! I told him no, it was not clear and I would do what I just did again! He went on to tell me, I was too stupid to help anyone in chemistry and teaching the students was his job. He lost his temper, as did I. He told me if I could not follow his instructions, we were going to the dean's office right then, and I would not be passing chemistry. In fact I was out of his class.

When people yell at each other; as he yelled at me there is really poor communication. Neither of us was listening or thinking clearly. Somehow reason returned and he asked me what I was going to tell the dean about my removal from chemistry class for not following his instructions. I told the chemistry teacher, I would just say that some people do not have common sense. When I saw three students passing open beakers of sulfuric acid over another student and then over your head too, I just had to stop what I was doing and talk to him. I told the chemistry student his method of passing acid was unsafe, because if the beaker slipped from his grip or you raised your head up or stood up you would have knocked the beaker of acid out of their hands and onto your head. The chemistry teacher then said to me: "*They did what!*" So I told him again. We never went to the dean's office. I went back to class. The incident was never mentioned by either of us ever again. Yet I did pass a very difficult Chemistry of Pollution class!

In all honesty, the chemistry teacher was very good. It was a very difficult and complex subject. We would get into the finer details of mercury poisoning from industrial waste getting into the food chain via fish and shellfish in the bays of Japan to the calculation of explosive yields on different tactical nuclear weapons. If you asked any of his students to talk about the many forms of pollution caused by man, I am sure every student could have intelligently discussed numerous pollution problems and discussed the finer points about the environmental consequences.

WHAT I LEARNED IN MY ATTENDING COLLEGE LESSON

I was not a smart student. I just did by best and hung in there doing all my assignments and turning in my homework. I didn't give up after being told that I was too stupid. Now, as Chief Laboratory Analyst, I've analyzed water and wastewater for twenty three years. It was "stick ability; not quit ability" which got me through college and to graduation day. In the end, it is persistence and not giving up which will lead you to succeed. Graduating from college does not guarantee you a job. It does not mean you will earn a lot of money. What college does do is when going for a job; you are a little more likely to be given a chance at the job you are applying for than a person without a college degree.

LESSONS AS A SEAMAN:

I tried to get several jobs after graduating from college but everywhere I turned I hit a stone wall. Then I went to downtown Baltimore and tried to get work at the Seafarers International Union. Now in all the lessons I am creating for myself life lessons that I chose to experience or learn. To get this job, I would need thought followed by action on my own accord. Had I not wanted to return to sea for more life lessons then I would not have gotten this job.

LESSION IN BULLIES RETURNS—THREE TIMES.

The first ship I worked on was a heavy lift ship the S. S. Transcolorado. This ship is designed to lift heavy cargo. A typical voyage might take us to England, France, Italy, Turkey, and Spain then back to the United States. While on this ship the "Bully's Lesson" returned again. I guess this was just a test to see if I understood the lesson. The first bully lesson was given to me by a seaman in my room who thought he was tough. There were a lot of tough men on that ship and he may have thought he was tough but if push came to shove, and that is what happened, he barely survived his fight.

This bully had the habit of showing everyone his knife and throwing it everywhere. He had threatened to kill me about half a dozen times, but he never really scared me. Unless he pushed me further, I just felt it was not worth my time and effort to break his legs. The old steward saw him threaten to kill me because I had not done the bully's work in addition to my own which I had completed. The old steward, who was about 65 years old, told me that he would have a talk with him. I told the old Steward I would take care of it if the bully pushed me further. I never got the chance as the old steward talked to him first.

While the bully was throwing a large bag of trash over the stern of the ship one night, the steward grabbed him by the back of his pants and belt in one hand and the back of his shirt collar in the other hand and heaved the bully over the hand rail right behind the bag of trash he had just thrown. With the old steward holding him face down over the middle of the Atlantic Ocean the steward talked to him about his unacceptable behavior and about how he had better change his ways if he had any desire to live any longer. Had the bully given the old steward any problems, he would have been instantly dropped into Ocean, falling into the churning propeller wash off of the stern of the ship. The bully was crying in fright, begging for his life and for a second chance and the steward decided to give him one.

On any merchant ship the stern is a very noisy place. The propeller is churning the water and vibrating everything on the stern. This vibration, in turn, sets the cans of paint and everything else to rattling. The noise on the stern of a ship is so loud that a person could scream and unless you were within fifty feet no one would hear anything. During one of my voyages, while I was in the stern of the ship, down in one of the storerooms a seaman tried to rape me. The seaman was bigger than and easily twice as strong as me. He grabbed me first by my wrist, and I told him to leave me alone; then I broke his grip with a move I was taught in karate making a fist and using an upward movement against his thumb which released my hand. The man continued the assault, grabbing me just below the throat at the top of the collar of my shirt with his right hand. I placed both of my hands on top of his right hand and did a wrist twist using my hands to turn his arm clockwise forcing his face down to the floor. I told him to leave me alone again and released him. Had he used force against me a third time I would have reacted violently doing my best to break one of his arms or legs.

He left me alone and never tried to rape me again. Literally he stayed out of my way.

Another seaman liked to walk up behind me and slug me in the kidneys. One day, the bully walked up and slugged me in the kidneys by complete surprise, and my Korean Karate training just flowed into action without my even thinking about it. As soon as I was slugged twice in the back, I pivoted and did a front snap kick into the bully's stomach. As my foot came back, I landed in a fighting stance ready to continue defending myself if he continued the attack. He left the mess hall and never hit me for fun again.

There was only one other time when the bully's lesson returned again and that was about ten years later when going to the bathroom in a restaurant. A big man grabbed me by the arm, and I again broke his grip on me. He grabbed me again so I had to break his grip on my arm twice. I was angry at the attack, and angry at myself for not hurting the man when I felt he would have definitely hurt me. I guess I was getting slow in my old age having not used karate in years.

What I learned in the lessons about bullies is that sometimes it takes force to stop an attack and everyone needs to be trained in self defense or weapons training sufficient to protect your life!

LESSON: THOUGHT, FOLLOWED THROUGH WITH ACTION IS CREATIVE. WISHES CAN COME TRUE—THE SHARPS RIFLE.

While working on the S. S. Transcolorado, I saved the cash to buy the Eastern Rose Silver Mine on 6th street in Leadville, Colorado. I was always interested in mining and prospecting and I thought this property up in the mountains would be a beautiful place to build a house and a good central base to prospect from when I was not on a ship. When the ship returned to New York after the end of its voyage,

I planned to get off the ship and take a vacation using some of my vacation time.

Before we arrived in New York, one of the seaman told me his dad owned a gun shop. He showed me his dad's catalog showing a selection of weapons. The seaman was trying to generate a little extra business for his dad and knew that most of the seaman getting off the ship would be paid thousands of dollars that they would just be waiting to spend. There as I lay in my bunk looking at the gun catalog, near the last page was a brand new Sharps 45-70 rifle!

I read and reread the description of the Sharps 45-70 rifle. I read how they used higher quality steel, how they improved the rifling twist, added sights you could raise up for long distance shooting, and made a tighter, safer breach seal than the originals to prevent blow back. It was a very nice Sharps rifle. I recalled my wish or dream to own one of these rifles back when I was still in high school. I remembered the effort I made trying to get one, and the trouble I narrowly avoided. I had the cash to buy the rifle, and I smiled. I acknowledged that, in fact, one wish I had made many years ago was effectively coming to pass. However it was no longer important to me. I acknowledged it, smiled, and let it pass! It is a nice feeling though to see that your wishes can come true.

WHAT I LEARNED IN THE LESSON IN THOUGHT FOLLOWED BY ACTION IS CREATIVE

Wishes can come true. I remembered creating the thought that I wanted a Sharps rifle when I was a teenager. This was followed through with action on my part. Now while I recalled the earlier wish and acknowledged it, the rifle was no long important to me. The Sharps Rifle lesson was that if you really want something / like any reasonable goal and you work and save for it then it can come to pass. Certainly, many years had passed by before my wish came true. I considered my wish fulfilled the day I saw the catalog and had an abundance of money with which I could have purchased the Sharps 45-70 rifle. I could have easily afforded the rifle as I had thousands of dollars on me at the time of the ships payoff in New York. I smiled at the thought that this wish had come true for me.

LESSONS I LEARNED BY RETURNING TO SEA:

The merchant marine's pay allowed me to buy the land in Colorado. It was the beginning of my move out West where I was going to experience a second phase of my life lessons as a prospector and tracker, but I did not know this yet.

The bully's lesson had returned again. The outcome was different than the first three times, because I had taken the time and made the effort to learn Korean Karate. I also felt the bully had created the lesson which took him to the brink of death. Possibly his Guardian Angel was trying to get through to him and convince him to change. The bully went on to go ashore in many ports getting in fights, which I felt he worked hard to create. Once he walked into a bar in Germany and with eight empty tables he walked up to the table where one U. S. Special Forces soldier was sitting and yanked out his chair dumping him on the floor telling the soldier he was sitting in HIS chair. When the bully left the bar he went out the closed front door of the bar head first! The bully came to me on the ship and told me, "…. everyone always picks on me!" He asked me to go back and get his $150 leather coat which was still in the bar. I told him I would if he gave me $250 to cover the damages I was sure he did to the bar! I told him I would return any of his cash that I did not need. I guess he did not want his leather coat that badly, as he was afraid to go back! You should remember that the bully created the lesson he chose to experience when he pulled the chair out from under the soldier when there was a bar full of empty chairs.

Certainly I never recommend deliberately picking a fight with a U. S. Army Special Forces Green Beret.

The S. S. Alex Stephens was the next ship that I worked on board. On this ship I worked as an ordinary seaman. Aboard this ship I encountered the worst dust storm in my life. While out in the Red Sea a high wind blew east off the deserts of Egypt carrying sand. The wind was blowing sand at about 40 to 50 miles per hour. When the sand hit your face or hands it stung you because it was traveling so fast. Visibility was less than 500 feet. I had always expected to encounter sandstorms in the desert southwest but I had never expected to encounter a sandstorm out at sea.

The return to Norfolk, Virginia marked the end of my voyage aboard this ship. I had asked my brother to buy me a full size pickup truck as he had more experience than I in negotiating a low price. I had told my brother to use my checkbook to write a check to pay for the truck. I had saved enough money to buy a truck.

When I got off the ship in Norfolk, my brother was standing on the dock with my new blue and white Chevy pickup. I drove that truck for the next ten years. It is a nice feeling when you can buy a pickup and just pay cash for it and not have to worry about making bank payments.

LESSON IN RELATIONSHIPS WITH THE OPPOSITE SEX:

I started dating a neighbor girl whom I liked a lot. She was always very nice to me, and I enjoyed her company. She had two children whom I got along with, and I thought of settling down with her. We had grown up in the same neighborhood and got along very well. Some times when I did not know what to say, she would ask me to tell her a story about my being at sea. I would launch into the story and she would scoot on over beside me acting all interested in my story. Before very long, her hands would be caressing me and my breathing would be getting very rapid.

Shortly thereafter I would forget where I was in the story and never finish it. I can still recall taking walks with her on wide paths in the woods, with the autumn leaves turning yellow, brown, and red. As we walked together down the paths in the woods the leaves would make a rustling sound as we walked and talked about our ideas and plans. Sometimes we held hands as we walked, sometimes we just walked beside each other, but my senses were very alive and aware of her presence since I can still clearly recall her in my memories thirty years later!

When I got off the merchant ship, I was thinking of marriage, building a house, and settling down with my pretty next door neighbor. But when I arrived at her house, I found that she had found a new boyfriend while I was away at sea! I guess the thoughts of how well we got along and of marriage were only in my mind and not hers or else my long time away at sea had allowed her to forget me in her heart.

WHAT I LEARNED IN MY RELATIONSHIP WITH THE OPPOSITE SEX: RELATIONSHIPS TAKE A JOINT EFFORT BY BOTH SEXES.

If one person no longer has an interest in making the relationship work, it will very quickly fall apart. While I thought I had a good relationship with this woman, clearly in her mind and actions (for thought followed by action is creative) she considered the relationship over!

When she told me she had met another man while I was at sea, she had put my belongings out in my truck. I came to the realization our relationship was over. So after a ride to town to replace a dead battery in my truck; I drove out of her life and have never seen her again!

Since I had been ashore awhile my money was getting very low. I needed to catch a ship. About this time, I had a chance to get a job aboard the Zapata Patriot, a tanker hauling oil and diesel fuel. I caught this ship out of Annapolis. A small launch took me out to the ship. We ran coastwise along the eastern sea coast of the United States for little while then went overseas to Europe. As I traveled the seas on the Zapata Patriot, I thought about how ironic some names can be.

Zapata was a Mexican Patriot who was simply before his time. Zapata wanted land reform in Mexico. He felt that each Mexican should be entitled to his own plot of land to farm. The land should not just belong to a few wealthy men. The majority of Mexicans had to work for the rich landowners as servants. Zapata was murdered by a company of Mexican Army soldiers under a flag of truce on direct orders of the president of Mexico! I thought it very ironic that the ship was named Zapata Patriot when he was murdered by government forces because the Mexican government had no intention of honestly carrying out land reform. Often it is a lot easier to speak well of the dead than get along with the individual in real life!

On the Zapata Patriot, I visited Italy, Turkey, The Suez Canal, India, Singapore, and I got off in the Philippines. In the Philippines, I caught a jet to Japan and then another jet back to New York. I tried getting another job on a merchant ship several months later but the economy had fallen apart. The jobs were just not to be found and so I found myself moving out West. I loaded everything I owned into my Chevy truck and headed west to Leadville, Colorado. Here I tried to get a building permit to build a small barn/shed that I could live in and work out of while prospecting in the mountains.

LESSON IN PAYING FOR WORK: A DRIVEWAY

I wanted a driveway into my property, and so I paid a man who said that he would use a bulldozer and put in my driveway for $650. He said that I had to give him $250 up front and that would cover his labor. Then he needed $200 to rent the dozer. I paid that too. When he finished I could give him his $200 profit on the job. The man absconded with the $450 of my money and never did any work!

What I learned in the driveway lesson is three in one: first get your agreements in writing! Secondly, I should have used a licensed contractor or the actual man who owned the bulldozer. It was a mistake using a man who just told me he knew how to run a bulldozer. The third lesson was I should not have paid for the work until the job was started and underway or even better when it was completed!

LESSON IN HONOR AND KEEPING YOUR WORD:

I went down to Taos, New Mexico to do some prospecting and meet the prospector Larry Campbell. While west of Taos, I met Dave Walker, a retired U. S. Army Colonel. Dave was Larry's neighbor. I liked the area and decided to try and buy some land out by Dave and Larry. The Colonel offered to sell me two building lots for $1,000. 00I told the Colonel I did not have the money on me, but I would go up to Leadville, Colorado and get the money for the land and return in two weeks. The Colonel and I shook hands on the agreement and I left to get the money from my bank in Colorado.

While I was gone, other people in Taos learned about the offer to sell me two building lots for $1,000. 00 so they offered Dave Walker $2,000. 00 for the lots Dave had promised to sell me! When I returned ten days later, I paid Colonel Walker the $1,000 we had both agreed and shook hands on. The Colonel told me that if he had not given his word to me and shook hands on the deal, he would have taken the higher cash offer. But since he was a man of his word, here is the land deed to the two pieces of property.

LESSON IN HONOR AND KEEPING YOUR WORD:

What I learned in dealing with Dave Walker was that his word and honor were more important than making a quick buck. **As you** go through life, some people have honor, integrity, and keep their word. Many individuals lack these qualities. Each person (and this includes YOU) has a free choice to set their standards high, or let them fall down into the gutter. Where you set your standards will affect the quality and integrity of the individuals you attract into your life. The choice is YOURS; so I hope you chose wisely! When tracking a trail through the mountains, or looking for a boot filled with gold (treasure hunting), the standards you set for yourself will affect the people you attract around you. Like will attract like — that is one of the primary rules of life! If you are dishonest, you will attract dishonest individuals all around you. So why not set your standards high, and attract men/women of honor, and integrity and who will be honest with you and stand by you to the limit of their existence! Are these not the friends and partners that you would dream of working with? So make it happen!

THE LESSON IN OWNING / BUILDING A HOUSE:

With the land I purchased west of Taos, I built a small 24 X 24 foot house. It was a 576 square foot house with two bedrooms, a bathroom, kitchen and small living room. I lived in this house many years.

THE LESSON I LEARNED IN OWNING AND BUILDING A HOUSE:

The money I saved up from working at sea enabled me to build the house. This house sheltered me through life for many years. One needs to save their money for a rainy day or one's goals in life; if one is determined to reach one's goals. By building the house myself, this enabled me to have sufficient money to complete the house. Should you choose to build a house yourself, you will have a mighty sore thumb as you learn to hit the nail on the head instead of the thumb and finger holding the nail. If you persist, you may have a nice home like I did which sheltered me through many storms in life.

LESSON ABOUT WOMEN:

As work was scarce around Taos, I decided to join a prospector I knew who was working up on the Yukon River panning for gold. While up in Alaska, I was over at a trapper's cabin. They had a problem with a grizzly bear, and they wanted to kill it. Shiloh and I agreed to help kill the bear and we took off with the trapper to track down and kill the bear.

The trapper had a very pretty 14 year old daughter, Susan who told me that they had taken off down the wrong trail. She told me the grizzly bear most often took the high trail above the log cabin where they lived. So I accompanied her up the high trail chasing after the grizzly bear with Susan leading the way through the forest and I followed behind carrying my 7mm Mauser rifle.

Well we never saw the grizzly bear, but before I got off that mountain at sundown, I could sure tell you that Susan and I enjoyed kissing each other! That night, she was all I dreamed about! Whenever we were out that way I always dropped in to see Susan. Before I left Alaska that fall, I told her parents that I wanted to marry their daughter and they agreed to the engagement but I would have to wait until Susan got older before we could get married.

About six months later, Susan's mother told me that I needed to send Susan a plane ticket so she could fly down and marry me. I got some help from my dad for the plane ticket and Susan flew from Alaska down to Alabama to marry me. As Susan was under age to legally marry me, we took her parents letter giving consent for our marriage and went to see a judge. The judge talked to me first, then he read Susan's parents' note, and finally he talked to Susan alone for awhile before he agreed to marry us. We were married by a judge in his courtroom. Susan was 14 and I was 28. Susan was the love and delight of my heart.

About two and a half years later, just before Thanksgiving Holiday, I asked Susan what she wanted for the Thanksgiving dinner as we needed to go shopping to buy the food we would fix for dinner. Susan told me: "Get whatever you feel like fixing for your Thanksgiving dinner; I am going over to XXXX's house for dinner and I will not be back as I am spending the night with him." Susan told me she wanted a divorce—I still very much wanted to stay married to her. I will not tolerate my wife sleeping with other men. It tears you apart inside when your spouse is cheating on you! I worked as rapidly as possible to get us the divorce. The divorce was completed the next month and the attorney's office charged me about $150 for the divorce and $100 in filing fees and court costs.

WHAT I LEARNED IN MY LESSON ABOUT WOMEN:

When we were in love, our time together was very nice. I have some wonderful memories of the good times we had together. I do not focus on the bad times; nor on the end when Susan no longer loved me. Yet when she no longer loved me and did not want to be with me; our relationship and the lesson ended. You have to let go when the lesson is over. Try to take some good memories with you; and when you leave I suggest you take the high road. Do not try and hurt your spouse, treat them with dignity, respect and honor. I am saying just treat them the way you would like and deserve to be treated!

LESSON IN WORKING FOR DISHONEST PEOPLE OR BEING CHEATED ON THE WAGES YOU EARNED.

Boy, this lesson keeps repeating itself—when will I learn? To support my wife and I; I did forestry work or whatever work was available. We lived in a small camper on the back of my Chevy pickup truck. We slept in sleeping bags and cooked our meals on a Coleman stove. The work we did was very hard work. We would get up early, have breakfast and start planting trees from daybreak to sundown. We were paid on average three cents for every pine tree that we planted. Sometimes we were honestly paid for the work we did. Sometimes we were cheated by the landowners we worked for.

Once we worked for a multimillionaire in Texas. He owned lots of gas and oil wells and thousands of acres of land. We were hired to plant hundreds of acres of land which took seven tree planters about three weeks. The agreement was that if the Texas Forestry Department inspected the work we did and passed or approved our work then we were to be paid. The Texas Forestry Department came out and inspected our work and approved us for payment. After we completed the job, the multimillionaire came out and told us that he did not plan to pay us; unless we planted about sixteen acres of land—literally several thousand trees for FREE! We were all so broke and desperately needed to be paid, so we allowed the multimillionaire to cheat us out of time, money, and labor!

WHAT I LEARNED PLANTING TREES--ANOTHER LESSON IN WORKING WITH DISHONEST EMPLOYERS WHO CHEAT THEIR WORKERS.

When you tolerate people cheating you it cuts you like a knife. You do not want to work or associate with individuals who have no honesty, dignity, nor honor! Just because a person has the financial ability to be honest certainly does not mean they have the character you would expect. There was no need to cheat us; yet this millionaire did it just because that was his character. He simply lacked honesty, and integrity. When you work for individuals lacking in honor, honesty and integrity, you are accepting less than what all individuals should set as their standards, and the results cut you in your spirit just like a knife cutting your skin.

LESSON IN WORKING AT THE STATE PENITENTIARY IN SANTA FE:

In 1980's, I worked at the State Penitentiary in Santa Fe. It was not a nice place to work. Certainly you do not want to commit crimes which land you inside the penitentiary because it is not a nice place to be. While I was working there neither the guards nor the inmates' behavior was above reproach. Inmates were murdered in the prison. Some guards were men doing their best in difficult situations, while some guards were insane or should have been locked up themselves; as they were not very nice people.

While working at the prison, I would sometimes sit and talk with the prisoners or the guards for hours to help pass the time and stay awake through the early morning hours. One guard told me he became a Correctional Officer because his nerves were shot. He had become a nervous wreck. He used to make a living stealing high priced cars like Mercedes, Jaguars, and other expensive cars. His income as a car thief was $80,000 –$120,000 a year. The correctional officer told me it was very difficult to adjust to the low pay of honest work as he now only made about $14,000 a year.

The officer then told me that he could not steal cars anymore because when a police car came into view he wanted to just open the throttle wide open to get away since he did not want to be caught in the stolen car. But he knew that if he did not act natural and could not calmly talk with the police when he was pulled over, he surely would be arrested! ! So finally he just could not be calm anymore, so he got a job as a correctional officer watching over the criminals who had been caught.

Another correctional officer told me about his treacherous wife who was trying to kill him. He told me how she would turn into a wolf as he was sleeping in bed with her. He would see her open her jaws with her long teeth ready to tear out his throat! He told me that already three times, he had jumped out of bed and run to the kitchen and grabbed the biggest knife he had, and then he ran back to the bedroom to kill his wife who had turned into a wolf. But his treacherous wife would just turn back into a sleeping woman and he realized, he could not slit her throat when she had used her witchcraft to turn back into a woman— he would just have to kill her when she was a wolf. The officer told me he was not sleeping very well as he constantly was awaking at night to see if his wife was a wolf or a woman! The correctional officer was terrified of his wife so he could not sleep at night.

Sometimes the correctional officers patrolling the penitentiary would fall asleep in their patrol car—one woman officer came out of her tower to awaken an officer who had fallen asleep under her guard tower. She propped the door open with the flash light (the watch towers doors are self locking) then walked around to the patrol vehicle and opened the passenger door. Next she picked up the shotgun on the seat beside the sleeping correctional officer who was snoring away. Then she walked around to the driver's open window and shoved the shotgun barrel into his mouth awaking him as she said to him: "You're dead. You axx hole! "She had clearly awakened the officer. He had soiled his pants before he realized who held the shotgun!

I remember joking with one officer and telling him that he must have been off hunting rabbits with his shotgun as one night because he missed his turn and drove off into the sagebrush sound asleep until the noise and the bumpy ride awakened him.

The cars the outer patrol drove were unsafe. For instance, my car had a heavy exhaust leak and thirty two points of impact (it was heavily damaged), the doors flew open on the curves or if you hit the brakes hard. The car the high ranking officers always assigned me, as I drove through the winter, had no heat—but I always kept the windows wide open because the exhaust smell was very bad. It could be 20°F outside, as I drove the car around the outer fences of the penitentiary, in winter with snow on the ground, but my windows were open so the exhaust did not kill me. I think they wanted me to quit, so they gave me a car with no heat and a bad exhaust leak into the car's interior, even though there were many new vehicles parked which I was not allowed to drive. One correctional officer died driving these unsafe vehicles. He crashed into the fence and died of a blood clot. I personally believe it was the carbon monoxide from the exhaust which caused the accident. His death was not an accident it was stupidity or a reckless indifference, in not correcting the exhaust from entering the vehicles.

While working in the penitentiary, I had prisoners who were mean and would try and kill you for no reason at all. They would attack you from the back and throw a one pound can at the back of your head to try and bust your skull in. By throwing the can at your back, you would not know which prisoner threw the can as you walked through a dorm room with 80 prisoners. Some of the prisoners are insane or so dangerous they should never be let out!

One night on vehicle patrol around the outer perimeter, I checked on the front gate to the penitentiary and the front correctional officer was gone! The lights were out at his guard post, the door was wide open and when I called out his name repeatedly no one answered me. First I looked everywhere I could see from my vehicle and I saw or heard nothing. Then I got out of the vehicle with my shotgun and walked around the position post from about 25 feet off to ensure no one was hiding behind the outside walls. Slowly, I approached the post and looked in the windows and saw nothing. I walked in, pushing the door to the corner wall and got about four to six steps into the post when I heard a scream behind me as the door flew closed and someone rushed me. I dropped to one knee, raised the shotgun to the center of body mass and pumped a round into the chamber of the shotgun I carried. It was like everything was moving in slow motion. I would have killed the individual moving towards me screaming, but the government had trained me in the use of the Remington 1100 automatic shotgun, the pump action took me almost a second longer to fire. As my finger moved to the trigger, the moving target that I was just a second from killing moved into enough light that I saw a correctional officer uniform! He froze as he saw me positioned on one knee with the shotgun aimed for his stomach, and heard the round chambered to fire. The end of the barrel was 18 inches from his stomach and my finger had already moved onto the trigger! His idea of a practical joke almost ruined my day—I would have had to explain why I had killed him! I was within one second of killing the correctional officer; as my finger reached the trigger and ended his practical joke on me!

I left the penitentiary shortly after my nose was broken by a guard who had thrown a dead battery at me. The radio battery hit me in the face, breaking my nose and sending me to the emergency room. Before they took me to the emergency room, I filled out an accident report. I was to fill out two more accident reports in the days that followed as every report I wrote was always "lost." Finally workers' comp denied my claim as I had failed to fill out an accident report!

LESSONS I LEARNED WORKING AT THE NM STATE PENITENTIARY:

Lesson 1: You do not want to be in prison; it is not a nice place.

Lesson 2: Some people are mean and will try and kill you for no reason at all.

Lesson 3: Some people will try and kill you from ambush.

Lesson 4: Some people are insane, be careful of them.

Lesson 5: Prejudice was very common and not very nice.

Lesson 6: Some people are fools; and do not think about the consequences which can arise out of their practical jokes like the shotgun in the mouth or rushing an armed officer carrying a shotgun at night.

Lesson 7: Many of the individuals I encountered there lacked honesty, honor, andthey had no integrity. They were not nice people you want to be with.

Lesson 8: Sometimes in life you take a job to achieve short term goals. This job wasvery good to me in that it enabled me to repair my truck and overhaul the engine which had well over 200,000 miles on it. By saving my money I was able to get a generator so I could have electricity in my house west of Taos. In addition I was able to catch up on some bills and pay them off. This work enabled me to put food on the table and some cash in my pocket.

LESSONS THAT I LEARNED FROM
MY NEIGHBOR JERRY:

I encountered Jerry when I made my first prospecting trip out West in the early 1970's. I knew I would be rich if only I could be as good a prospector as Jerry. Jerry had grown up in the Great Depression. He was a small time hoodlum who knew about a murder by the gangsters he worked for and associated with. He liked being with gangsters as it made him feel important and gave him a sense of power.

His enjoyment of being with crooks and getting a bargain on stolen merchandise disappeared when he was served a subpoena to appear before a Grand Jury. He was bragging about how tough his friends were, and about a murder he witnessed, when he was heard by an undercover police officer. Jerry was his own worst enemy. By bragging about who his friends were, it made him feel important. When his "friends" heard that his mouth had gotten him an invitation to appear before a Grand Jury, they decided to close his mouth and let him swim with the fishes, with some concrete blocks chained to his feet. A friend warned Jerry he better split town if he wanted to avoid getting killed!

Jerry went home, packed a bag and told his wife and kids that he would send for them as soon as he got a place that they could live. Jerry never returned for his wife or sent for her. After all, as Jerry told me many times, every man knows it is a woman's fault if she gets pregnant; they do it just to trap a husband. If his wife wanted food on the table she would just have to go out and get a job. She and his kids were not going to take advantage of his labor any longer. They would just have to support themselves.

Jerry headed to Florida to get a job in Miami but he ran out of bus money in a small town in South Carolina. Here he got a job as a foreman at a two thousand acre truck farm growing vegetables for the cities up North. The blacks at the farm were paid a penny for every bushel basket of tomatoes they picked. In the fall, when watermelons were harvested, the black employees working out in the field were given a nickel for every twenty-five water melons they harvested. Jerry would count the baskets of produce each worker harvested and on pay day he would take a wheel barrel full of pennies, nickels, and dimes and pay the employees.

Jerry had an easy job and made $10 a month. The farmer that Jerry worked for had a pretty daughter, and soon Jerry was courting the farmer's daughter, Sara. The farmer told Jerry it was fine with him if he married his daughter but if he got her pregnant and intended to abandon her in a family (pregnant) way, he would kill him with his shotgun and have the blacks bury his body out in the backwoods.

Several months later, Sara told Jerry that they had to get married now as she "was in a family way" due to Jerry's nightly visits to her bedroom. She told Jerry that everything would work out because her dad liked Jerry. Sara told Jerry that if he asked dad for permission to marry his only daughter, that she knew her dad would say yes. Jerry told Sara that he had to wait until pay day. Then he could go to town and buy a ring. Only then could he come back and properly ask Sara's dad for permission to marry her.

Sara knew Jerry loved her as he told her so every night when he slipped into her bed. Jerry would whisper into Sara's ear how she was the only woman for him. He always told her how much he loved her and how he would always be there for her. "You know baby, I could never live without you. You are everything to me, baby." Sara was so happy that Jerry took the news of her being pregnant so well. It just went to show her how much Jerry loved her.

On payday Jerry got his pay and told Sara he was going to town to get her a wedding ring. When Jerry got to town, he got the first ride out of town, of going west! Jerry had lied to Sara so she would not tell her dad she was pregnant until he had traveling money to head west. Jerry felt he was having a run of bad luck. First, he fled New York to avoid the Grand Jury he had been subpoenaed to appear before. Here he had a good job paying him good money when that Sara had deliberately gotten herself pregnant. A man has his needs and Sara had just tried to trap him, he knew it was all her fault he lost his job.

Jerry got a series of rides to Oklahoma where he jumped into an empty box car with half a dozen men heading west. There on a freight train, he met a hobo named Steven. They got along so well that Steven invited Jerry to travel with him. Near dinner time the freight slowed down at a train station to add and remove some boxcars of freight. Steven and Larry jumped off the train to find a meal. Steven told Jerry, just follow my lead, pretend we do not speak or hear what they say, and this always works to get a free meal. Jerry followed Steven up to a house where three women lived. A mother and two daughters met the two men when they knocked at the door.

Jerry and Steven motioned to the three women that they were hungry, pointing to and circling their stomach with their hands, and then they made motions like chopping wood. The mother felt sorry for the two men and she led them over to the woodpile where both men started splitting up wood into small pieces for the wood cook stove. After both men had split wood for two hours, the mother invited the two men who had it so hard in life not being able to speak or hear, into the kitchen for dinner. They all sat down for dinner, bowed their heads in prayer, and the oldest daughter said grace. For dinner, they ate a big bowl of beans along with some bread and jam with each having a glass of water.

The mother turned and said to her daughter, "You know it would not be too bad having a husband who could not talk. They certainly would not be complaining all the time or telling you what to do." As she talked, both men ate in silence pretending that they did not hear or understand a single word being said. The mother then said to her daughters, "If you were picking a man to be your husband, which man would you select and why?" The oldest daughter said she liked Steven the best as he was a good hard worker as he split firewood. The younger daughter said she liked Jerry the best as he was more handsome, and she liked skinny men.

When dinner was over, the two men walked to the kitchen door and bowed to the three women and said, "That was a very nice dinner." The three women were speechless for a few moments. They were embarrassed at what they had said. Then the three women threw a pan of dishwater at the men and chased them out of the kitchen with a broom.

In California, Jerry got a job driving a delivery truck delivering bread, cheese and sausage. There he met a nice single woman named Cathy and they began dating. It was not long until Jerry began telling Cathy that he loved and needed her so much. She was the type of woman he dreamed of meeting and settling down and having a family with.

Jerry told Cathy that it was time she started taking care of her man's needs. Jerry told her, "We can start doing it now because you know that I love you and you are the only woman for me. You know that I will always be here for you, honey. I will always take care of you." Before long, Cathy was expecting a child. Cathy told Jerry we need to get married now because soon everyone will know that I am pregnant. Jerry told Cathy, "Well let me save a little money for the wedding license and a wedding ring and we will get married in two weeks." Cathy was so happy that Jerry would stand by her and help her in her time of need. She knew Jerry was the right man for her and he would keep his promise to take care of her.

Jerry was ready to pack his bags and hit the road. By saying he would marry Cathy in two weeks; she would never suspect that he would be gone this Friday when he got paid. Women were always getting him fired from his jobs. Well he certainly did not intend to let Cathy trap him with that story that she was pregnant. A man had his needs, and it was Cathy's tough luck if she had gotten herself in a family way. What did she expect? He certainly was not going to stick around and be a father or pay any of her medical bills! Thursday night, after getting his needs met in bed with Cathy, while she took a bath, he quickly packed a paper bag with his most important possessions and set them outside where he could grab the bag on his way to work in the morning.

The next morning Jerry grabbed his bag after walking out the door on his way to work. Well, it was Friday, and it was good he was getting paid since he needed some traveling money. At work, Jerry was mad at Cathy for costing him a good job, and trying to trap him into marriage. Women were always taking advantage of him. Jerry was just so mad at all the women in his life costing him job after job. As Jerry sped down the road in his delivery truck, he took a curve at high speed and all four tires and rims collapsed. Jerry's boss fired Jerry. It was the second delivery truck accident he had. Jerry told his boss he did not know what happened as he took the turn at 15 mph. "It certainly was not my fault the wheels collapsed." Jerry's boss fired Jerry anyway. Two delivery truck accidents were just too much. Jerry counted the $5 he had been paid and smiled, that would keep him fed until he got another job.

Jerry was always willing to help out woman; as long as it did not cost him anything. Jerry went to a brothel. He told his friend Mark that he could have any woman there for free. Mark bet him a dollar that he couldn't. Jerry went over to the madam who ran the brothel and told her he wanted a girl and asked what she cost. She told him $2 for fifteen minutes. Then Jerry picked out a woman to have sex with. As they walked up the stairs and into her room, he told Sally that he was a friend of the madam and she said he could have her for free. Sally said no one gets it for free. Jerry asked her if the madam told her it was ok; then was it ok with her. She said, "Yes, if the madam says it is okay." Jerry went back down to the madam and told her he wanted to talk to her for a minute. So Jerry and the madam walked into her office to talk. In the office, Jerry told the madam that Sally said his equipment below the belt did not look right to her so she would not have sex with him.

The madam told him to drop his pants then she would look at them. After looking at him, Jerry asked the Madam if she would tell Sally that it was okay. When they walked out of the office, the madam hollered up to Sally that it was okay. Then Jerry went up the stairs to the room with Sally. As they were in bed together, Sally told Jerry that it was very unusual for the madam to give it away for free. The madam was real tight with money. Later he smiled as he collected the dollar for his winning bet from Mark.

In Colorado, Jerry met an excellent treasure hunter in Trinidad. Bob was an excellent treasure hunter and over a campfire dinner Bob invited Jerry to go treasure hunting with him. Bob was a top notch researcher who carefully researched stories about outlaws. When Bob's research indicated that there was enough data or information to make it possible to find where the outlaws may have hidden their loot, then Bob invited Jerry to accompany him to the site which they then searched with metal detectors.

Jerry's first share of a recovery was seven thousand dollars. Jerry was ecstatic. This was great. During the depression, Bob had begun writing about his treasure hunting to put bacon and beans on the table. Even though Bob no longer needed the money from his writing about treasure hunting, Bob continued to write as he enjoyed trying to help people. Bob often would write about his treasure hunting but he would use the names of his friends as the individuals who had made the recovery. Bob talked about the treasures that his friend Jerry was recovering in his books; and soon Jerry was enjoying the attention he was receiving even though he did not have the ability to make a treasure recovery on his own.

Jerry took his share of his first recovery with Bob and took his $7,000 and spent it all in two days. Bob gave Jerry the strong box that came off the stage coach that was hauling the gold and silver coins. As Jerry did not have space in his camper for the strong box, he gave it to the first hardware store on the north side of the main business street in Trinidad, Colorado. The strong box was on display behind the cash register, up on the wall for many years for all the customers to see. When I saw the strong box, I asked the hardware store owner what was in it and who found it. The store owner told me that was the same question that he asked the old man I had come into the store with.

Jerry had given him the strong box. When Jerry was asked what was in the strong box he replied: "Just use your imagination." Jerry had purchased a new pickup truck, a camper, and two bottles of fine scotch whiskey from the contents of the strongbox. Yes, this is the life he dreamed about. Now he was a professional treasure hunter. After consuming his first bottle of whiskey, he lit up a cigarette to smoke and he began drinking his second bottle of whiskey. Jerry woke up with his camper on fire. His life was saved by the fire department that pulled him out of his burning camper on the back of his pickup truck. All was lost in the fire!

Jerry's second treasure recovery was when he accompanied Bob to a Spanish Mission Church in New Mexico. Bob had learned in the New Mexico State Archives that a gold miner had been heading back east with his gold he recovered in the California Gold Rush. The padre at the mission had cared for the dying gold miner but he passed away with pneumonia. Bob's hunch was that as the padre was taking care of the dying miner, he probably hid the gold in the mission until the next of kin could come and claim the money.

So Bob, Jerry, and H. H. visited the church about midnight. They broke into the church through one of the side windows. Bob, Jerry and H. H. quickly searched the church interior and located a loud metal target under the altar. They quickly tore up the mission floor as the dogs in the pueblo began barking. There under the church altar lay a broken wooden box with iron bands which had rusted away. As they picked up the wooden box the box broke apart in their hands. Gold coins tumbled everywhere! Bob told Jerry to find something to carry the gold coins in. In the dark the only item that Jerry could find was the padre's robe, which Jerry grabbed and filled with coins.

Out the church window climbed H. H. , Bob and then Jerry. As Jerry was last, he carried all the gold in the padre's robe. As he was crawling out the window, the robe caught on the window latch. Jerry just pulled harder on the padre's robe and tore the robe again, scattering the gold coins everywhere.

All three men were doing their best to pick up the gold as quickly as they could before someone in the pueblo came out to investigate why the dogs were all barking. As soon as they had the coins gathered up, they all took off running to where they had hidden the car. The three men recovered just under $3,500 in gold coins from the old Spanish Mission Church. This gold was then sold for $18,000 at a coin store. Jerry's share was $6,000. Jerry spent it in a week, paying bills and buying a pickup truck.

Jerry's third and last trip was up into Taos Canyon. Here, Jerry had heard from an old Indian living on the Taos Pueblo that a Spanish pack train from the 1700's was coming down Taos Canyon towards Taos, when the pack train was ambushed by Indians. Jerry went to Bob with the story and Bob was able it deduce where the pack train went when attacked. After searching a number of side canyons, the site where the pack train was ambushed was located and the silver bars were found.

Bob then drove into the site with his pickup truck and they took out three loads of silver bars during the night. They hid them in a new site that they could return to if they needed extra money. The original site still had some silver bars remaining that they could not load into the truck that night. Neither Jerry nor Bob ever returned for the remaining silver bars, they thought the risk was too great since they drove past several houses that night.

Jerry sold his silver bars for $1,800 which he used to start building a house out on the mesa west of Taos. One night when Jerry had had too much Scotch Whiskey he accidentally set his house on fire, again. A very nice neighbor, Colonel Walker, found Jerry out on the snow covered ground and rushed Jerry to the hospital, saving his life.

Jerry was not always the nicest man. He had no doubt when he knocked over a child in the supermarket that he was in the right. After all, the child did not rush to get out of his way. Jerry felt that children should get out of the way of adults and if he knocked a few children on their bottoms; well he was just teaching them to respect their elders.

Jerry kept from starving by living off his social security check. Throughout his life, Jerry bummed around or did cash jobs which did not contribute to his social security benefits. When Jerry got social security it was the minimum amount, just $200 per month. When he was 70 years old, he went and applied for food stamps to make his cash go further. Because Jerry was not nice to the people who issued his food stamps, they in turn were not nice to Jerry. They told Jerry that he only qualified for $12 in food stamps per month! They also told Jerry that the federal guidelines they had to enforce required him to apply for three jobs a week if he wanted to receive his $12 in food stamps next month. Jerry never went back. It cost him $5 to drive to town. If Jerry drove to town once a week and applied for three jobs it would cost him $20 in gas to receive his $12 in food stamps.

When Jerry was in need of help he would make promises he had no intention of keeping. For example, he promised three of his neighbors (I was one of them) that he would show them an old Spanish gold mine up at Cumbres Pass, in Colorado if they helped him get his house ready for winter. We all pitched in and hung solid wood doors on the front and back of his house. We loaded two tons of coal into the back of his truck. Then we unloaded it in his back yard. We also helped him cut and split three cords of wood, and helped him build the framework for his water tank to sit up by the roof line of his house. Keep in mind that when you are helping Jerry cut a load of wood up in the mountains or load and unload two tons of coal; that the way Jerry helps you, is to stay out of your way. Jerry does not cut the firewood or load it in the truck. He just drives up into the mountains and you just have to find the dead standing tree, cut the tree down, block the wood up, load up his truck, then unload the truck at his house, split the truck load of wood and stack it!

After we did all the work Jerry had asked us to do in our agreement, he made up a big lie about why he couldn't take us to the gold mine. He said he would like to keep his promise and take us to the Spanish gold mine but it was hunting season now in Colorado so it would not be safe to go with all the hunters out shooting. Maybe, he said, we can go next year. A week later, we found out it was not hunting season in Colorado. When we took Jerry the Colorado hunting regulations with the hunting season clearly indicated and showed him that his excuse was a simple lie, he refused to honor his word. After we did everything to complete our part of the agreement, Jerry refused to honor his side of our agreement.

THE EIGHT LESSONS THAT JERRY TAUGHT ME WERE:

1. Jerry created his own luck; so Jerry was his own worst enemy. His drinking lead to his burning down his house, truck, and camper.

2. Jerry was dependent upon Bob for every treasure he recovered as he was unable to make a recovery on his own.

3. Jerry would go through his share of the treasure caches that were recovered in just two to five days. He spent his recoveries rapidly like a drunken sailor.

4. If you looked in detail how Jerry treated the women, children, and individuals in his life, he did not treat them with dignity, respect or honor. He was not an individual anyone should hold up as a role model. If you work with an individual who does not treat others with dignity, respect, or honor, then be forewarned they will not be someone you want to associate or learn from.

5. If an individual does not keep his word to you, then you do not

want to go treasure hunting with him –if a person has no honor— walk away from him!

6. Jerry always felt it was acceptable to cheat and lie to women—no one deserves this kind of behavior of being cheated and lied too!

7. Jerry deliberately made promises he had no intention of keeping; he cheated me and others out of our time and labor. No one deserves to be cheated, lied to, and have their time and labor stolen from them.

8. Jerry lacked honesty, integrity and honor.

LESSON IN WORKING AT THE POT CREEK SAWMILL:

I worked at the Pot Creek sawmill near Taos for about a year. Work at the sawmill was very hard and I worked at the most difficult job in the sawmill, the green chain. On the green chain, the rough cut lumber was removed from the conveyer and stacked in piles by the size of the lumber. So 2x4, 2x6, 2x8, and 4x12 would each be stacked in separate piles of lumber. I came home from the job so tired that I only had energy to take a shower and fall asleep. Then after I slept for several hours I got up and ate dinner.

WHAT I LEARNED FROM WORKING AT THE SAW MILL WAS SIMPLY THAT HONEST WORK CAN PUT FOOD ON YOUR TABLE.

I certainly was not cut out to work at this job and I was getting too old for it. I physically had to move tons of lumber every day. Fortunately this job was one which paid my bills and put food on the table until I found a job more suitable for me.

LESSON WITH MARIA:

Maria was a nice Hispanic woman that I met while both of us were simply surviving. We both had very little money after paying our bills.

But by pooling our money we were able to manage to get by. Maria had two sons named Paul and Juan. After three years together we had a daughter Dancing Wind.

It was a struggle trying to get the boys to school. Neither son wanted to be in school, and soon they both dropped out of high school. Of the two boys, Paul was the one who always thought of the needs of others and would always try and help out. Unfortunately, Paul would not wear his seat belt. I literally told him a hundred times to put on his seatbelt. He would lay it on his lap, but never fasten his seatbelt. One night, he had had a few beers and was out driving with his friends. Paul rolled his truck on a hard turn and died when he rolled his truck over. The other teenagers were fine. I always felt that if he had just worn his seatbelt he would be alive today. But every day individuals make choices, some are good and some are poor. My son Paul's choice not to wear a seat belt cost him his life.

Juan is an individual who thinks of himself first, last, and always! He has one main priority in life—himself. When his car broke down, it was usually the result of something stupid Juan did deliberately. Juan decided to drive his car into the water at Abiquiu dam. Using the boat launch ramp he deliberately drove his car into the lake. Water flowed into his car and shorted out the electronic brain on his Nissan Sentra. Juan's solution was then to cheat his sister Dancing Wind out of her college money. While Maria and I had no money, he knew that we had put aside U. S. Savings Bonds for Dancing Wind's college. Juan told us he would lose his job if he did not go to work. The only way to fix his car was for Maria and I to cash in all our daughter's U. S. Savings Bonds to pay for a new electronic brain for his car. Juan told us that if we cashed in Dancing Winds's bonds he would pay us from his paycheck from his job starting the next Friday. Maria and I cashed in our daughter's college money to fix Juan's car. As soon as his car was running he refused to repay a penny of his sister's money!

When Juans's car's water pump gave out and he needed his car fixed, Juan told us he would lose his job if he did not show up for work due to his car being broken down. At this time, Maria and I were planning to celebrate our wedding anniversary by taking an all day train ride on the Cumbres Toltec Steam Train going from Antonio, Colorado to Chama, New Mexico. Maria and I could just barely afford the trip but it was a very special occasion for us. Juan told us that he would pay us on Thursday. So we would have plenty of time for us to buy the tickets on Friday so we could take the trip we planned. So we agreed to lend him the money for our train tickets to repair the water pump on his car.

Juan got paid from his job on Thursday afternoon. But once Juan got paid, he had no intention of going home to pay us back the money we had lent him to fix his car. Come time to go to Colorado on Friday morning, we could not find Juan! He and the money he promised us simply were not to be found! Maria, Dancing Wind, and I went to Kentucky Fried Chicken to buy us a lunch to take on the train, and we also took a cooler with drinks for the train ride. I had about $100 in available credit on my VISA card so I was able to take my wife and daughter on the trip as I promised them.

Two days later when I saw Juan, I asked him what happened to the money he promised to repay us so we could take the train ride. Juan told me he just did not have any money! Juan told us that after he ate out at Red Lobster, paid for drinks at the bar, went out to movie and dinner with his date, and got a hotel room for the night, he simply did not have that much money left, so he simply could not pay me. He told me he needed the remaining money to pay for gas going to work and his lunches out!

When Juan's truck was going to be repossessed after he had fallen behind on his payments he came to us and asked for $500 to make two payments on his truck. Since Dancing Wind and I both wanted to keep some horses on Juan's land, we told Juan to clean his lot and build us a corral, and we would give him the $500. Juan told us he had to have the money today as they were coming for his truck NOW! He would clean the lot and build the corral "this week! "It has been over fifteen years and "this week" has not yet come!

Juan and his girlfriend got a trailer and put it on Juan's lot. Sandy and Juan were not very happy with Maria and I since he said, "We were not making our fair share of their trailer payments! " It seems to me that it was their land, and their trailer, and Juan and I were in fact paying our fair share—*nothing*!

After Juan and Sandy fell six months behind on the mortgage payments for the trailer that they were living in, Sandy and Juan asked Maria and I to take over the payments to prevent them from losing their trailer. I told them that I did not have any money, but I would talk to the bank if they wanted to sell me the trailer and land, and I would see if I could borrow the money.

The banker in Espanola told me that he sees this happening all the time. He told me that if I took over the loans and purchased the land and trailer that unless they had moved out, allowing me to immediately move into Juan's and Sandy's trailer, that I would be making the payments the rest of my life while I supported another man and woman living in the trailer! If I immediately moved into the trailer then they would move into our paid for trailer –" just temporarily until we find a place" --in other words, until we died! So think long and hard about which house you want to live in and which house you want to give them! The Banker went on and told me if I gave them the $500 to pay the electricity, or the $2,000 to pay the water bill that they found no reason to pay all year that they would pocket the money and no bill would be paid! Tell them that the bank needs the deed to the land first, as well as the trailer payments contract with whom they purchased the trailer. The bank will also need a letter from each utility on how much is owed to resume service. You need to get all the legal papers and bring them into the bank. Then we will talk to the mortgage holder and see if anything can be worked out.

That night when Juan came by, I told him the bank needs all the legal papers to the house and land signed over to the bank. This really got Juan mad when I told him that the banker needs the legal papers to the house and land. Then he asked me for the $2,500 to pay the electricity and water. I told Juan that I did not have any money at all. The only way I can get any money is for the bank to get title to the house and land—then they may loan me the money; but I will not see a single dollar of the money as it will go to the mortgage holder on the house and the bank will pay it directly to whom is owed money like the taxes, water, electric, and the trash. When I talked to Juan that night, he stormed out of the house all furious with me, slamming the door on his way out! Apparently he had no intention of conveying the legal title to the land or the house! They just wanted us to pay all their bills! Several months later the mortgage holder repossessed the trailer and now the lot is vacant.

THE LESSONS JUAN TAUGHT ME ARE:
1. Juan thinks of himself, first, last and always.
2. Juan will tell you what he thinks you want to hear.
3. Juan will not keep his promises to you.
4. Juan is poor at managing money.
5. Juan lacks honesty, honor, and integrity.

LESSON: THE SUMMER HORSE RIDING CAMP LESSON.
Dancing Wind is Maria's and my daughter. She is one of the loves of my life. When Dancing Wind was about thirteen, she wanted to ride horses. I suggested to Dancing Wind that if she could find a summer

camp which had horse riding that I would try and come up with the money to send her to the horse riding camp.

Dancing Wind found a camp for teenage girls who wanted to ride horses, and I could just afford to send her to camp. My wife Maria hit the ceiling. She was furious with me! Never had I seen her so mad at me in my life. She did everything she could to prevent Dancing Wind from attending the horse camp. While I worked full time and paid the bills, Maria only worked part time. Since I had to work, I asked Maria to drive Dancing Wind to camp. She refused. She accused me of trying to murder my daughter. My wife was convinced our daughter would fall off the horse and die. She said: "Never again will you pull this nonsense on me! "I felt that professional riding instruction with other teenagers would be an excellent learning experience for my daughter—and it was. I did not back down on this major argument with my wife.

Maria had dozens of reasons why my daughter simply could not go to summer camp for a week. We cannot waste the money that it cost to send Dancing Wind to horse camp. They might sell the girls into slavery. They will not feed the girls and Dancing Wind could starve to death. I was just trying to murder my daughter. Why did I hate my daughter so much that I wanted her dead? What if my daughter is kidnapped while at horse camp? You're just trying to starve her to death. You always hated her, and now you're trying to kill her. I asked Maria to drive her to the summer Horse Camp. Maria refused to drive her to camp. Maria thought if she refused that would settle the matter, with Dancing Wind staying home. I took the day off work and drove Dancing Wind to summer camp.

Dancing Wind went for a week of riding at the Girl's Horse Camp in Grants and had a wonderful time. I would recommend it to any parent who can survive the arguments from their spouse, concerning sending your child to summer camp. She was also exposed to social skills as she interacted with other teenage girls. Besides having a lot of fun riding horses, my daughter also learned a lot about caring, feeding, and riding horses. If you asked my daughter, I am sure she would say she will never forget the experience and her memories will last a life time.

WHAT I LEARNED IN THE LESSON OF LEARNING FOR DANCING WIND

Some people's fear can prevent or block new learning and life experiences. I would not back down on this argument with my wife because I thought it would be an excellent learning experience for our daughter. Years later I can look back on this decision, and I still felt I did it right. As I was proof reading this portion of the book, Dancing Wind gave us a phone call from Colorado where she now works. She was letting us know that she was planning to go horseback riding this weekend with some of her friends.

LESSON: SWIMMING.

I wanted my daughter to learn how to swim, so I would take my daughter to the swimming pool sometimes. I felt the best way to avoid drowning is to teach a child to swim. Again Maria accused me of trying to murder my daughter. She asked me why I was trying to kill my daughter. "Do you hate Dancing Wind that much that you want to kill her? " she would ask. I told her that our daughter is safer learning to swim than not knowing how to swim. I did not back down in the argument with my wife. Dancing Wind is now a very good swimmer.

WHAT I LEARNED IN THE SWIMMING LESSON WITH DANCING WIND

Parents can have two complete opposite views of what is a safe activity, such as swimming or riding a horse. Maria's view was never get near the horse or the water. My view point is teach the child to safely ride the horse or swim in the pool. I would have gone a lot further than I did and taught my daughter "Drown Proofing"—and after she mastered the technique, then I would have liked to teach her to swim with her hands tied in the water, then with her feet tied, then after she was comfortable swimming with her hands or feet tied and swimming I would have gone further and taught her to swim with her hands and feet tied with rope. But I did not go as far as I would have liked as I was afraid that the government authorities would have taken my daughter away from me if they saw us together in a swimming pool and my daughter had her hands tied together and her feet tied together. Certainly my wife would have been convinced that I was actively trying to murder my daughter. I just wanted my daughter to master the skills involved in swimming so she can always handle herself safely in the water.

LESSONS: WEAPONS

I wanted my daughter to understand weapons and how to use them safely. So I spent time teaching my daughter how to safely use both rifles and handguns. I do not want her to be afraid of weapons, but I also wanted her to understand how to use a weapon if needed for self defense.

WHAT I LEARNED IN THIS LESSON ON WEAPONS:

One can safely teach your child how to use a weapon. You just need to teach at the teenager's pace of learning. Certainly if you are not very familiar with weapons I would recommend professional weapons instruction. My daughter and I have gone out into the mountains and shot at paper targets for hours enjoying ourselves.

When I look back on the time my daughter and I spent together, I have three regrets. I did not yet have the financial resources to take her canoeing on the rivers. Nor at that time, did I have the financial resources to take a vacation with her, and teach her diving with a hookah rig. Most importantly I would have also liked to instill into both of us an attitude, a philosophy, and a determination of persistence, in the endeavors one embarks upon in life!

RED RIVER LESSON:

My next job was working in Red River. I worked for the Town of Red River for 5 years. This job ended when I reported what I thought was a crime to the FBI. I had gotten a letter from an engineering firm asking questions of a technical nature. The questions revolved around "the handling, melting, and shaping of kilogram quantities of plutonium". The only situation to the best of my knowledge where this series of technical problems occur is in the manufacture of a tactical nuclear weapon.

When the FBI failed to come see me in what I considered a reasonably prompt manner—and they had plenty of time to get off their rear end and get on a donkey and ride the hundred miles north to come see me, if they could not find a working car. I took the light blue embossed document and sent it certified mail, return receipt requested to the United States Central Intelligence Agency in Langley, Virginia.

The next day after I reported it to my boss, I was promptly fired from my job. I was told that if I come back on the property (Town of Red River) I will be arrested. So far as I know the FBI, often called the Cabbage Patch Dolls did nothing! So now you that the CIA calls the FBI Cabbage Patch Dolls, because they sit on their fat bottoms and can't do anything right! You saw this same level of competence prior to 9/11 when one Special Agent wanted to look at the contents of a computer that belonged to one of the terrorists prior to the attack, and the FBI supervisors stonewalled the request.

I took a trip to California, and when I returned I had another accident. While my wife and I were fast asleep our house suddenly caught fire in the middle of the night. The Fire Marshall later told me that the entire floor of our house, 20 X 30 feet, had instantly combusted. Only the smoke alarm woke us up in time to get out of the house alive! Maria had asked Pat to install the smoke alarm the day before our house burned down. When we went to use the phone to call the fire department, my wife told me the phone was dead; it simply did not work. Maria and I grabbed our daughter Dancing Wind and fled the house as it was engulfed in flames. We drove the car over to the neighbors' house which took between one and two minutes. As we stood on their front porch knocking on their door we looked back at our house and there were flames coming out every window!

WHAT I LEARNED IN THE RED RIVER LESSON:

1. I handled the "document situation" poorly. I should have made many electronic copies of the "document" and ensured that they were in several safe locations. Certainly there wasn't a safe location to keep the documents in my house.

2. I acted too hastily, suppose it was an honest job offer from and engineering company, I certainly would have not been hired by any company with whom I had called the FBI about my job offer.

3. I had thought that the FBI was competent. Their actions to me seemed less than competent when one is talking about a breach of the nuclear surety of the United States.

4. Certainly I thought that if the FBI could not find the keys to their car they would be able to get off their bottom and get on a donkey and ride one hundred miles north in ten days!

5. An employer, like the Town of Red River which fires an employee who reports a crime—is showing no support for the employee. They are lacking in honesty, integrity, respect, and honor.

6. Throughout all these life lessons; again and again, it keeps recurring time and time again: *dignity, honor, honesty, integrity, respect, and competence.* When you associate with or work with people that lack integrity, dignity, honor, honesty, respect, competence it is always asking for trouble and problems.

LESSON: THE CITY OF ESPANOLA

After losing my job in Red River, I got a job with the City of Espanola where I have worked for over eighteen years. When I first came to work for the City of Espanola Waste Water Treatment Plant, I was the only non-Hispanic working there. During my first year, I remember that new Carhartt jackets were purchased by the city for the waste water employees. Every employee got a new jacket except me. Once when I was in one of the locked store rooms, I saw they had three brand new extra jackets there that no one was using, but I still didn't get one. When I had to work during the Thanksgiving holiday, a Thursday and Friday to do the laboratory test in the lab I was given two hours of overtime. To get the two hours of overtime pay, I worked twelve hours that Thursday and Friday. It was many years before was finally paid twelve hours of overtime pay for the twelve hours I worked during a Thanksgiving holiday. When I went on vacation I was the only City of Espanola employee; to the best of my knowledge, that their boss had written on my vacation request: "If Barton Thom is one day late returning from his vacation, I recommend he be terminated."

For the first two years when I answered the phone I regularly got phone calls for my boss inquiring about the job opening for my position in the lab. I would just take the callers name and number and post it on my boss's door where I left all his phone messages. It certainly leaves one with an insecure feeling about your job when your boss is regularly advertising your job as open to anyone who applies for it.

I stuck this job out and slowly over the years I was treated more fairly. I got along very well with my last boss Carlos and the crew that worked with me.

WHAT I LEARNED IN THE LESSON OF WORKING FOR THE CITY OF ESPANOLA

Looking back on this lesson in life I was in a slow transition phase learning to prospect, track and writing stories of our adventures. The good part about this job is it put food on the table. This work covered my family and I with medical insurance, it paid the bills—usually, while I learned tracking and prospecting. I retired from the city and I have a nice pension which still pays my bills.

There were days when this job was rough but it is persistence and stick ability which enabled me to regularly bring home a paycheck. Finally after many years I was always treated nicely. This job supported my family and helped pay for my daughter's college education. I retired from the City of Espanola with a nice pension because I stuck with this job. As I type this I am down in Port Isabel (by South Padre Island), Texas finishing up the manuscript on two of my books.

BANKRUPTCY LESSON:

After the fire, I spent a lot of money putting purchases on credit cards. For example the day after the fire, I found out I did not even have a pair of tennis shoes to my name. When my family fled the house as it burned down around us, I put on one tennis shoe from one pair of shoes and one tennis shoe from another pair of shoes in my haste to get out of the burning house. My good jacket with $500 dollars of emergency money was in the living room of the house when it burned. The electricity in the house had gone out when our house caught fire, and I could not find the jacket in the dark so this money was lost.

The day after the fire, I purchased $1,200 in clothes at Wal-Mart. I am talking about two pair of jeans, two shirts, socks, shoes, underclothes, belt, jacket for myself, then my wife and daughter. The insurance reimbursed me $165 for all my clothes lost in the fire. When I went to buy a suit to go look for a job, I spent over the $165 which was the total amount I had been paid to reimburse me for all my clothes.

The spending continued with Paul asking to borrow some money for a truck so he could work and make money. I told Maria I would lend him $2,500 and go with him to look at trucks. Maria went with Paul and purchased a used truck for $4,500 with the transmission going out. As soon as I heard the truck running, I knew the transmission was shot—and the truck should have never been purchased! Then I told Maria and Paul they needed to find a discount transmission shop in Albuquerque to repair the truck. Maria and Paul then drove to the dealer in Santa Fe which charges about twice as much as the transmission shops. Before the truck left the dealer's shop, the repair bill was $2,400! The loan I agreed to make for $2,500 had already grown to $6,900 and it was all charged on the credit card. Then Paul did not get a job or make truck payments so I could pay the credit card! Instead in one month he charged $200 in gas to Maria and me. My budget was busted!

I purchased a commercial fishing boat in Coos Bay, Oregon. I didn't look at the boat before I bought it, but I thought I might like to get into the commercial fishing industry. The engine did not run. I tried repairing the boat, but since I wasn't around to keep an eye on it, the other boat owners who needed a part would come steal it from my boat. I never got the marine engine running but I poured more money into the boat which would be lost in the fast approaching bankruptcy.

I looked for a house on Coos Bay and I found a water front house down by the marinas that was all run down, but that could be purchased for $29,000. The house and yard were a mess, weeds grew high in the yard, and the paint was peeling everywhere on the outside of the house. Inside the house there were barrels of fishing supplies, floats, and nets. To walk inside the house there were narrow rows or aisles that one could follow. Literally the entire interior of the house was packed with tons of fishing gear, tools and supplies of a commercial fisherman. The extremely poor appearance of the house scared off any possible buyers. I had taken out my pocket knife and checked dozens of places—the cedar wood the house was built of was structurally sound. To me the house was love at first sight!

If one walked the 70 feet through the waist high weeds there was a gentle slope down to the water. I saw where I would plant fruit trees. Yes this was the best buy I had ever seen on nice water front property since my dad had purchased 1/3 of an acre of water front property near Annapolis, Maryland on Weems Creek for three thousand dollars.

I talked with my mother and she said she would lend me the money—on one condition. The one condition was that Maria agreed to the purchase also and co-signed on the written loan agreement. Maria absolutely refused to agree to buy the house or move out to Oregon. She was furious with me that I could have even thought she would ever live with me in such a run down piece of junk. She wanted to return to New Mexico immediately!

Shortly after returning to Abiquiu, Paul died in a rollover accident in the pickup truck he was driving. I used the cash advance on my credit cards to pay for the funeral. I was using the cash advance just to make the credit card minimum payments, since they had climbed to more than $400 a month. I realized that I was so far buried in debt that I even used the cash advance to get money to pay for an attorney to file bankruptcy!

WHAT I LEARNED FROM THE BANKRUPTCY LESSON:

1. When you purchase items on credit cards that you do not repay you will lose that item. Certainly everything I purchased on the credit card from the boat to the truck was lost.

2. When you borrow money you cannot repay you are headed for trouble.

3. You will either lose the item, it will be stolen from you, or some other manner that results in your losing whatever you acquired. So in the end, no benefit is gained by your action.

4. Call it karma, call it "what comes around goes around"--but rest assured there will be balance in the end!

5. I still use credit cards all the time now—but unless there is a very good reason for it; I do not charge more than I can pay off at the end of the month

6. An exception to paying off an item at the end of the month; in my life recently is my wife's car needed $1,400 in repairs at the shop. I certainly did not have the money saved for the repair bill, so I am making larger payments on the credit card to get the debt paid off as quickly as possible.

7. I have a high credit score now; my banker told me I am grade "A" paper now.

LESSON WITH MY DAUGHTER AND I SPIRIT TRACKING WITH DAN:

One of the best lessons, certainly the lessons I enjoy and cherish the most are the lessons and time my daughter and I spend with my *friend* Dan. Dan taught us about tracking, prospecting and life. *Dan is an individual with dignity, honor, honesty, integrity, and loyalty.* He does not teach or talk about some lofty idea or goal, but he teaches by example. When he is teaching lessons about tracking; incorporated in those lessons will be lessons about dignity, honor, honesty, friendship and loyalty. He may be teaching by showing it to his student, or by showing it to a spirit that has died one or two centuries ago.

It is in the lessons with Dan, my daughter and I often experienced what I thought was impossible. I have learned how to reach out into the future and bring a thought or concept into reality. Helping my daughter attend and graduate from New Mexico Tech with a degree in Civil Engineering is one example. My daughter was taught by Dan many spiritual concepts from tracking a spirit or ghost as described in *The Treasure of Francisco Martinez* or the story *The Apache* to taking Spirits Home as in *Path of the Angels*. I considered the events which occurred in *The Treasure of Francisco Martinez* absolutely amazing. That we could help three German Priest return *home*, that water began flowing in the dry arroyo at the site where Francisco married Maria, that the Snow Pixies worked with us, that the deer communicated with Dancing Wind were just some of the miracles I witnessed. A second example of reaching out into the future and bringing your concept into the here and now are these stories your reading about Angels. Dan encouraged me to write the stories *Tracking with Angels, Flight of the Angels, Path of the Angels, Justice of the Angels* and many more. By example, he teaches and shows that goals can be accomplished. The adventures I have with Dan are like my spirit finally coming alive. Never would I want to go back to the way I was before I traveled the spirit trails with Dan. I learned so many lessons writing this book and while tracking with the Angels; though I have shed many tears; they are also the best times of my life.

If you can dream of meeting an Angel, he demonstrates to you that it is actually possible to meet one! Often he demonstrated to my daughter that she can track a trail that is centuries old, and *know* exactly what occurred along the trail she was tracking. When my daughter tracked a Spaniard, whose very life is an example of honor and integrity like Arturio (Arturio is discussed in more detail in the second book: *Flight of the Angels)*, who was murdered by assassins over a century ago, she knew where his mission was, where his camps were and even where and how he was murdered.

Arturio was a man of *honor* and he stood by *his word*. He could have rode out on a mule and escaped with his life. He could have packed a second mule with gold and took it too. Yet Arturio had given *his word*, so he stood against impossible odds. Arturio was a priest whom died in an attack by sixteen assassins from Abiquiu. I can still recognize Arturio's camps up in the mountains on sight, even though this honorable man lived a century before my time*! **When one spirit tracks a trail while working with one's Angels they are adventures one never forgets!***

Dan teaches of love and compassion for your fellow man by showing you that both in his actions and by example. Certainly I would not have known what to do or how to effectively handle the spirits that I encountered in *"Sand Creek –A Love Story"* without the help and support of our teacher and Dancing Hawk. In experiencing the events in my third book *"Path of the Angels,"* a lot of tears were shed. *"The Apache"* reflects as accurately as I can about my daughters tracking experiences in the Malpais and how those events with this treacherous spirit unfolded. *"The Treasure of Francisco Martinez"* details my daughters first attempt in negotiating with a spirit. There my daughter interacted with the spirits of three German Priests, and learned about how deer and people can communicate. This is the first time she interacted and worked with Snow Pixies and how they make snow. I never imagined that Spirit, through prayer, and Divine Grace can result in water flowing in a dry stream bed yet I saw it with my own eyes!

Each story in this book illustrates lessons that I have learned with the help of Dancing Hawk (my Guardian Angel) and Dan. We have had many adventures together, and each story represents a lesson. Through helping the spirits that I meet along the way, I have learned many lessons of the spirit. Another side benefit is that helping others always feels good. I really enjoy each new adventure, and *I want to share them with you and help to awaken a relationship between you and your Guardian Angel.*

When I wrote about my experience in "SAND CREEK-A Love Story", I wrote it, just as I experienced or called it—it is as factual as my Guardian Angel could convey it to me. This was my most difficult lesson, but one both Dancing Hawk and I needed to do together. It is a testimony to the skill of my teacher that he could send his student and friend to Sand Creek with just his Guardian Angel to accompany him. Sand Creek is a detailed account of my spirit tracking trail.

I had wanted Dan's help but he was unavailable to travel with me as he had urgent business on the other side of the world. I simply did my best at Sand Creek. I was very concerned about the results because I wanted to do it right. I shed a lot of tears at Sand Creek. Dan told me I did just fine, a complement coming from my teacher means a lot to me.

Dancing Hawk's request was completely unselfish as she had needed me to help take her two dearest friends Running Antelope and Morning Star *home* to GOD's *house* where they belong. Dancing Hawk helped walk me through it all, as we will continue to walk through life together.

I was requested by my daughter not to use her real name in these stories; I honored my daughters request. I used the name Dancing Wind, a word play on my guardian Angels name Dancing Hawk, as the main character in all my stories to show honor and respect to my Guardian Angel. Dancing Hawk accompanied me on all of the trails I tracked. Several of the stories or trails described in these stories were told to her by Angels she knows; giving you a view into some of the trails that trackers though out the southwestern United States are currently tracking. ***All the stories contained in this book on: "Tracking With Angels" are a gift to you! They show you that an imperfect person,*** *like you or I can work with Angels. They are a gift to you to help you connect to your Guardian Angel and teach you, that you too can interact with the Angel now sitting there beside you!*

Open your heart
Open your love
And you have the key
To heaven above!

Sand Creek — A Love Story

On the second day of February 1953, I was born in Dayton, Ohio and Dancing Hawk had chosen to be my Guardian Angel. For fifty-two years she has watched over me and helped me countless times asking nothing in return. She received no gifts, simple thanks, and for a very long time, I didn't even acknowledge her. I didn't show her my appreciation for the thousands of times she had tried to give me good solid advice and help me, because I didn't realize that I had an Angel helping me. Certainly being a Guardian Angel is a difficult task! I chose to honor her by naming the main character in my stories after her. I used a word play on Dancing Hawks name and called my main character Dancing Wind. These stories are dedicated to my beloved Dancing Hawk.

In the autumn of 2005, I learned of the presence of my Guardian Angel. As the leaves began to change color, I was also undergoing a change from the inside out. I became more aware of my Guardian Angel, and I began the first small steps of communicating with her.

Our first big breakthrough in communicating came as my Guardian Angel showed me her name. She began by placing pictures in my mind, of a woman dancing. She repeated this until she was certain that I understood that she wanted me to think about dancing. Next she showed scenes of a Hawk flying through the air. After I got the picture, she put them together. I didn't understand the exercise at first, but she persisted. I felt as if the new information had opened the flood gates to our communication, and now I knew her on a first name basis.

That winter, I began to work *with* Dancing Hawk. We began to help spirits who had become lost or trapped on the earth to return *home* to heaven with the help of GOD's Angels. Many times I worked with my daughter and Dan to help spirits to return home. In the story "Tracking Through Time" and also in the account in "Path of Angels," one can read about how spirits or ghosts who had become trapped or earthbound can be helped to return to heaven where they really belong--in GOD's loving hands.

As our spiritual teacher, Dan taught us to track trails that had been long forgotten. We also did some prospecting along the way. Often the trails we tracked were hundreds of years old. We encountered many spirits during our adventures, and we always tried to help them find their way *home*. Dan taught us in spiritual matters, prospecting and tracking. I believe that no trail is tracked by accident—there was always a reason for the trails that we chose to track. Often our Guardian Angels arranged or chose the trail to track, and frequently the reason was associated with a lesson I needed to learn. Many times the trail was tracked because my Guardian Angel knew that there were spirits along the old trail which needed help returning home.

As Dancing Hawk and I spoke more often, our conversations became easier and more frequent. One day, Dancing Hawk asked me for a favor. This was the first time in fifty-two years that Dancing Hawk asked me for anything. She asked me to go to Sand Creek, Colorado on her birthday, April 23. I asked her if I could give her a gift, and Dancing

Hawk requested *a Native American Indian doll, a red dress, and a red rosary.*
Yet clearly the most important request Dancing Hawk made to me, was
that I go to Sand Creek, Colorado on her birthday, April 23.

I sought each of the things that Dancing Hawk had requested. And
I immediately made arrangements for the trip. After a month I found a
Native American doll, but I felt that I needed to buy three. So in time,
three Indian dolls were purchased. I purchased a red rosary next. I
never found the appropriate red dress. I am just a man after all, and I'm
certainly not perfect. April 23, 2006 was fast approaching, so I checked
the local plant nurseries until I finally found two White Sage plants
which are sacred to the Cheyenne Indians.

I contacted Chuck and Sheri Bowen for a tour of the Sand Creek
massacre site. The Bowens gave me a tour of Sand Creek on April 23.
The Sand Creek site is on private land, the ranch of Chuck and Sheri
Bowen. It was very important for me to go out to Sand Creek on the 23
of April so I could keep my promise to Dancing Hawk.

The Bowens took me on a tour and showed me the numerous
battlefield artifacts they had carefully recovered and preserved from
Sand Creek, or the Big Sandy as it is referred to on topographical
maps. The Bowens told me about the solders that came up from Fort
Lyon. The U. S. Calvary had forced Robert Bent to guide them to the
Indian encampment. At six miles out from the Indian encampment
Robert Bent took the cavalry solders off the main trail and the party
veered east. Bent wanted to give the Indians camped at Sand Creek
enough time to become aware of the soldiers moving toward the camp.
Many Indians escaped the massacre because of this delay. Early in the
morning, Kingfisher, who was out checking on his horse, saw the
soldiers marching toward the camp. He ran back to warn everyone.

★★★★★★

It was November 28, 1864, and Dancing Hawk a young Cheyenne, was very happy. She was going to be getting married the next morning. Running Deer would be coming for her and she would begin a new life with her husband. Dancing Hawk and her mother were busy with preparations for the wedding. Her mother was excited about giving her daughter last minute advice before Dancing Hawk moved into her new tipi with her husband.

Dancing Hawk's two best friends Morning Star and Running Antelope, were Arapaho. Their family was camped south of her lodge on the Sand Creek. Morning Star was eight years old and her sister was five. Both girls were excited about their best friend's wedding. It had been hard for Dancing Hawk to find a husband because she was considered different from most other girls her age. Dancing Hawk occasionally had dreams of future events, and many young men avoided her because they were afraid of her gift. Even teenagers that were Dancing Hawk's age avoided her as she would tell them about a future event before it occurred. Her two young girl friends were also different like her so they got along very well together.

Dancing Hawk and Morning Star occasionally had a bad dream about the buffalo disappearing. In the dream, the herd of buffalo would turn into a herd of Blue Coats who would attack and kill their people. Both girls prayed to the Great Spirit that this would not happen.

The chief of the Cheyenne, Black Kettle had made peace with the soldiers at Fort Leon. The Cheyenne had turned in their rifles and been given an American flag to fly so that soldiers would know not to hurt them. They were camped at the Big Sandy Creek or Sand Creek as they called it. The camp was spread out over a mile along Sand Creek because there wasn't very much water. The water they had came from holes dug in the dry creek bed, and they used it for both people and livestock. Black Kettle had signed a peace treaty with the U. S.

Army. The army promised the land they camped on would be made a reservation.

Dancing Hawk did not like the white men because they had made this promise with the Cheyenne before. Years later they would take back the land they had given the Cheyenne. Every time a new treaty was signed, the Cheyenne were given less and less land for a reservation. The white men always wanted more and more land from the Cheyenne. Soon there would be no land left for the Cheyenne!

The white men would slaughter the buffalo. Often they would take only the tongue or the hide, leaving thousands of pounds of meat rotting on the ground. These white men had no respect for life; neither animal nor man. To the Cheyenne, the buffalo were sacred. The Cheyenne depended upon the buffalo for their very existence. The food the Cheyenne ate, as well as the hides to make the tipis which protected her people from the cold winter winds all came from the buffalo. While all life was sacred to the Cheyenne, no animal provided so much to feed and clothe her people as the buffalo.

★★★★

Dancing Hawk told me, *"The attack came at sunrise, the morning of November 29, 1864. Hundreds of Blue Coats attacked us for no reason other than we were Cheyenne and Arapahoe. The soldiers hate was so great that even though we had surrendered our weapons and were camped on the land we were promised for our reservation, they had come to kill us all."*

"They had promised us peace and told us to fly the American flag; yet at sunrise hundreds of soldiers opened fire on our camp with rifles and cannons. Rifle fire was everywhere; cannon balls were exploding in our village spreading death in their path. There was complete terror everywhere. The slaughter had begun. Why had they promised us peace then treacherously attacked us?"

"Running Deer rode up to my tent and told me to flee to the northwest. We

hugged each other for a moment with tears in our eyes. He told me to go now. Then he rode to the south to join the few warriors to try and slow the soldiers attack, so as many people in the village as possible could escape. I never saw my fiancé, Running Deer again."

"*Running Deer would join about twenty to thirty warriors that could ride, to try and slow the attack of the hundreds of blue coats. They wanted to try and buy, with their lives, as much time as possible for their families to try and get away from the slaughter the Blue Coats had come to bring upon the Cheyenne that day. For every warrior with his bow and arrow that rode out and tried to stop the Blue Coats there were twenty to thirty soldiers shooting at each Indian warrior.*

The Indian bow could effectively shoot fifty yards. The Blue Coats opened fired upon the Cheyenne and Arapahoe people from 200 to 500 hundred yards with their rifles and cannons. Very few of our Cheyenne warriors got close enough to even shoot an arrow from their bow before they died in the heavy rifle and cannon fire. None of the Cheyenne warriors who tried to slow the soldiers advance into their village lived. They all gave their lives trying to allow some of their families to escape."

"*As soon as Running Deer left me, I followed him to the south where the fighting was most intense. I went to grab my best friends who were in the Arapahoe village and take them to safety. I wanted to help Morning Star and Running Antelope escape. There was fighting and shooting everywhere. Cannons with grape shot / canister shot and round balls were exploding and bringing death everywhere. As soon as I found Morning Star and Running Antelope I grabbed the terrified girls' hands and started running to the north with them up Sand Creek. I tried to stay in the shelter of the cottonwood trees and willows growing along Sand Creek."*

"*I ran up Sand Creek to the northwest fleeing to get away from the soldiers. I ran with five year old Running Antelope in my left hand and eight year old Morning Star in my right hand. When Running Antelope fell I just pulled her, back up on her feet and we all kept running. I tried to save my best friends from* the slaughter going on all around me. As we fled north away from the soldiers we were in a race for our lives, but I heard the yells of the soldiers and their horses behind us."

"We could not outrun the five Blue Coats chasing after us. I heard the bullets flying all around us as the Blue Coats shot at us. But I would not let go of Running Antelope's hand until the bullet slammed into my back. I fell face first into the sand."

"I heard the soldier yell, 'I GOT ONE, I GOT ONE' as he got off his horse. The soldier handed his horse's reins to another Blue Coat. He got down on one knee and rolled me over. As I looked up at the Blue Coat I was angry. I could not understand what was going on, or why they would slaughter my people like animals."

"To my right, I saw a soldier swing his rifle butt into the head of Running Antelope smashing her head in. Then the Blue Coat pulled out a knife and tore off the scalp of my five year old friend."

"As the soldier who had shot me stood up, I saw the lust and excitement in his face and eyes as he dropped his britches. He dropped to his knees, pulled up my dress and entered me. I did not struggle or move except to try to breathe. Blood was coming out of my nose and mouth. I was drowning in my own blood as it filled my right lung."

"When the soldier was finished, he stood up and spit on me as he pulled up and fastened his britches. He saw the anger in my eyes. He then pulled out his knife and cut the skin holding the hair to my head. Then he jerked off my black hair scalping me."

"Then the Blue Coat stabbed me in the upper chest cutting a circle with his knife around each of my breast cutting them off me. I did not scream. I just coughed and choked on my blood and died. Then he cut a circle around my vagina; cutting my lower abdomen, legs and butt as he tore off my skin around my vagina. Later he would make a change purse to hold his coins when he was paid by the government."

"With my scalp, and my two dear friend's scalps the three Blue Coats would lie and tell stories in Denver about the three Cheyenne warriors they had killed at Sand Creek. Many men would buy them drinks in the bars to hear the story about the Cheyenne warriors that they had killed in battle."

"As I looked down at my lifeless body and that of my friends I realized that Morning Star had died beside me about twelve feet to my right. She had been ridden over by a Blue Coat on a horse killing her! He, too, had scalped and mutilated her body. My dear friend Running Antelope's scalped body lay a few feet south of me. She was just a baby, but they treated her just like me."

"I was so angry at what the Blue Coats had done to my friends. They were so young and innocent and they had just begun their lives on earth. Beside me these Angels came and held and hugged me. As I cried, they accompanied me to a Tunnel of Light, where I was filled with so much love and light. There were two Angels beside my friends, but they seemed lost in the nightmare continually replaying the last twenty minutes of their life, over and over again. I promised Morning Star and Running Antelope I would come back for them."

★★★★

"**This is my commandment. That you love one another as I have loved you. Greater love hath no man than this, that a man lay down his life for his friends.**" (*John 15, 12-13.*) Certainly Dancing Hawk gave her life trying to save her dear friends. You can ask no more of anyone than what Dancing Hawk did when she tried to save the little girls lives.

★★★★

About 142 years had passed before Dancing Hawk again returned to Sand Creek, Colorado. Love often means keeping your promises to the ones you love. Dancing Hawk was coming back to Sand Creek after 142 years to keep her promise to her two best friends. She decided to bring me along. Sometimes even Angels need help. Dancing Hawk wanted my help in taking her friend's *home* to heaven.

Dancing Hawk helped me choose sacred White Sage plants to plant in memory of the two Arapaho girls. I also brought a doll for each of them. I placed the red rosary with love, on the spot where Dancing Hawk had left her earthly body. With other Angels help, Dancing Hawk was able to stop her two friends from continually replaying the last minutes of their death. Then Dancing Hawk showed Morning Star and Running Antelope the sacred white sage plants and the Native American doll that she had brought as gifts for each of her friend's spirits. Eight Angels helped Dancing Hawk as she talked to her very good friends, about how it was now time to return *home* with the Angels.

As I drummed for the two girls, I also prayed for them and called upon the Angels to come and help come take the two girls *home*. A woodpecker and an owl nearby began setting the beat for me to drum. Both animals also wanted to work with the Angels to help the two young girls' spirits. Barton asked the two girls to follow him as he drummed and walked in a circle. Slowly Barton picked up the pace faster and faster until suddenly two new Angels arrived and stepped out from a white circular Door of Light. The two little girls saw their family inside the Tunnel of Light calling them home. In an instant, the girls, with their two Guardian Angels shot into the tunnel of light and were gone. Then the two Angels, one on each side of the door, followed the two girls into the Tunnel of Light. As suddenly as the Door of Light had appeared, it disappeared. When the two Indian girls' spirits had gone *home,* I stopped drumming. For a few minutes Dancing Hawk and I cried. A hundred and forty two years had passed since Dancing Hawk made her promise to her two dearest friends to come back for them. That is how true LOVE is.

Dancing Hawk's fiancé, Running Deer had also died at Sand Creek.

Running Deer was born again on the second day of February 1953. Dancing Hawk chose to spend her life with him as his Guardian Angel. That is how LOVE is. It swirls and flows all about and around even through time, and touches everyone you LOVE in a positive way!

Iwould love to hear from my readers. While I may not be able to answer all my correspondence you can be sure I will read all your letters. Should you wish to receive a e-mail of new books as they are published you can write me and send me your e-mail address. Any one who wishes to receive a free short story of Dancing Winds adventures can receive it via e-mail for the asking. The readers will need to be patient with me as it may take several months to answer your request as I may be out in the field tracking trails with my good friend Dan and Dancing Hawk.

I have written four books with stories of Dancing Wind and her friends. They are available on Amazon and also as a Kindle E-story, and their delivery time will be weeks faster than mine. If you like my stories please tell your friends or better yet give them your favorite book as a gift.

Barton Thom
trackingwithangels@yahoo.com
Dancing Hawk Press,
223 East Maxan St. # 107,
Port Isabel, Texas 78578
Tracking with Angels
Flight of the Angels
Path of the Angels
Justice of the Angels
Each book is 19. 95 and I will pay the postage in the United States.

Please remember Amazon and Kindle ship promptly, I take about two months at my Port Isabel, Texas address. Yet if time allows I will try and answer your letter. GOD SPEED, Barton

www.ingramcontent.com/pod-product-compliance
Lightning Source LLC
Chambersburg PA
CBHW060305100426
42742CB00011B/1871